Social Work with Children, Young People and their Families in Scotland

Transforming Social Work Practice – titles in the series

Collaborative Social Work Practice	ISBN-10: 1 84445 014 7 ISBN-13: 978 1 84445 014 5
Communication and Interpersonal Skills in Social Work	ISBN-10: 1 84445 019 8 ISBN-13: 978 1 84445 019 0
Effective Practice Learning in Social Work	ISBN-10: 1 84445 015 5 ISBN-13: 978 1 84445 015 2
Management and Organisations in Social Work	ISBN-10: 1 84445 044 9 ISBN-13: 978 1 84445 044 2
Social Work and Human Development	ISBN-10: 1 90330 083 5 ISBN-13: 978 1 90330 083 1
Social Work and Mental Health (second edition)	ISBN-10: 1 84445 068 6 ISBN-13: 978 1 84445 068 8
Social Work in Education and Children's Services	ISBN-10: 1 84445 045 7 ISBN-13: 978 1 84445 045 9
Social Work Practice: Assessment, Planning, Intervention and Review	ISBN-10: 1 90330 085 1 ISBN-13: 978 1 90330 085 5
Social Work with Children and Families	ISBN-10: 1 84445 018 X ISBN-13: 978 1 84445 018 3
Social Work with Drug and Substance Misusers	ISBN-10: 1 84445 058 9 ISBN-13: 978 1 84445 058 9
Social Work with Older People	ISBN-10: 1 84445 017 1 ISBN-13: 978 1 84445 017 6
Social Work with People with Learning Difficulties	ISBN-10: 1 84445 042 2 ISBN-13: 978 1 84445 042 8
Using the Law in Social Work (second edition)	ISBN-10: 1 84445 030 9 ISBN-13: 978 1 84445 030 5
Values and Ethics in Social Work	ISBN-10: 1 84445 067 8 ISBN-13: 978 1 84445 067 1
What is Social Work? Context and Perspectives (second edition)	ISBN-10: 1 84445 055 1 ISBN-13: 978 1 84445 055 1
Youth Justice and Social Work	ISBN-10: 1 84445 066 X ISBN-13: 978 1 84445 066 4

To order, please contact our distributor: BEBC Distribution, Albion Close, Parkstone, Poole, BH12 3LL. Telephone: 0845 230 9000, email: learningmatters@bebc.co.uk. You can also find more information on each of these titles and our other learning resources at www.learningmatters.co.uk.

Social Work with Children, Young People and their Families in Scotland

STEVE J HOTHERSALL

Series Editors: Jonathan Parker and Greta Bradley

LearningMatters

First published in 2006 by Learning Matters Ltd

British Library Cataloguing in Publication Data
A CIP record for this book is available from the British Library.

ISBN-10: 1 84445 031 7
ISBN-13: 978 1 84445 031 2

Cover and text design by Code 5 Design Associates Ltd
Project management by Deer Park Productions
Typeset by Pantek Arts Ltd, Maidstone, Kent
Printed and bound in Great Britain by Bell & Bain, Glasgow

Learning Matters Ltd
33 Southernhay East
Exeter EX1 1NX
Tel: 01392 215560
Email: info@learningmatters.co.uk
www.learningmatters.co.uk

Contents

Acknowledgements

A number of people have assisted me in different ways in producing this book. In particular, my thanks go to Gina Allan, Phillipa Berry, Janine Bolger, Ian (Milton) Crockatt, Aphra Fisher, John Hammond, Jackie Hothersall, Jo Hughes, Christine Jennings, Joyce Lishman, Terry MacLean, Alistair Stobie and Patrick Walker. Thanks also to other colleagues at Robert Gordon University for their forbearance.

I dedicate this book to my children, Jamie and Hanna. Thank you for everything.

Introduction

Social work with children, young people and their families is a very challenging area of social work practice. It is also one of the most rewarding, although its demands can make those rewards seem very distant at times.

This book focuses upon social work with children, young people and their families in Scotland. In this regard it is the first book of its kind, mapping out in detail the social work landscape as it currently exists in Scotland, drawing together a range of legislation, policy, research and practice evidence to present a coherent picture of Scottish social work with children, young people and their families in the wake of the recent Report of the 21st Century Social Work Review, *Changing lives* (Scottish Executive 2006a).

The book aligns itself to the requirements of the new (Scottish) Standards in Social Work Education (SiSWE) (Scottish Executive 2003a) which underpin the introduction of the new honours degree in social work and is consistent with supporting those requirements as well as the requirements of the Scottish Social Services Council Codes of Practice (SSSC 2005).

The book will be invaluable for all students undertaking the new honours degree in social work, as well as qualified practitioners already working in this area, as it offers a coherent picture of a very complex landscape. It will also be of use in relation to continuous professional and employee development, post-qualifying programmes of education and training and a number of other social care courses and settings. The text will also have great value as a source book for teachers, trainers and academics with an interest in this area as well as practice learning facilitators and a range of other professionals in health, education, the police and the legal profession.

Chapter 1 examines the legal and policy context within which social work practice with children, young people and their families currently takes place. This chapter sets out the parameters within which social work takes place, looking at the devolved Scotland of the 21st century as well as considering the historical development of law and policy and its contribution in shaping the current landscape. Due reference is also made to international influences and the unique legal system within Scotland. This chapter sets the context for your practice by emphasising the dynamic nature of the interaction of law, policy, people and practice.

Chapter 2 takes an in-depth look at the children's hearing system, unique to Scotland. This system, designed to respond effectively to children in need, whether they have offended or been offended against, is looked at in the context of its relationship to the social work task. Recent developments concerning the children's hearing are also considered in the light of issues around increasing levels of youth crime.

Chapter 3 looks at ways in which support can be offered to children, young people and their families. The chapter considers the role of discourses in social work which influence practice as well as looking at the types of services available and how these might be used.

Chapter 4 focuses on child protection, looking at the current frameworks in place to protect children as well as considering how these operate. What we mean by child abuse and neglect is considered and the impact of a number of influential inquiry reports is discussed as well as the findings of the recent Child Protection Audit and Review. There is detailed information concerning the processes involved in protecting children, with emphasis being placed upon the experiential elements of this most demanding area of work with children, young people and their families.

Chapter 5 looks at those children and young people who are looked after and/or accommodated by the local authority. Consideration is given to the issues which may lead to some children having to live in some form of substitute care setting and emphasis is placed on the ways in which practitioners can work ethically and safely with very vulnerable individuals.

Chapter 6 focuses upon collaboration with other professionals and with children, young people and their families. There is discussion on the wider issues around this theme with reference being made to the need for practitioners at all levels to be alive to the dynamics of collaboration and to respond effectively to this issue, rather than taking the passive approach to collaboration which suggests that practice of this nature should take place because policy-makers say so.

Chapter 7 looks back in order to look forwards. The chapter considers where social work has been and where it needs to go in the 21st century. The recent Report of the 21st Century Social Work Review *Changing lives* is considered along with commentary concerning some of the issues looked at by the Review team. The chapter also considers the importance of building capacity for sustainable change and, uniquely, locates this in a learning enhancement framework which seeks to involve children, young people and their families as active participants in this process.

Throughout the book there are a number of diagrams, tables and activities, all of which are designed to enhance your understanding of this challenging, fascinating and richly rewarding area of social work practice.

Chapter 1
The legal and policy context

A C H I E V I N G   A   S O C I A L   W O R K   D E G R E E

This chapter will help you to meet the following Scottish Standards in Social Work Education (SiSWE) (Scottish Executive 2003a: available at www.scotland.gov.uk/library5/social/ffsw.pdf).
Key Role 1: Prepare for, and work with, individuals, families, carers, groups and communities to assess their needs and circumstances.
1:1 Preparing for social work contact and involvement.
Key Role 4: Demonstrate professional competence in social work practice.
4:1 Evaluating and using up-to-date knowledge of, and research into, social work practice.
4:2 Working within agreed standards of social work practice.

Introduction

This chapter will take you through a number of important issues relating to the relevance of law and policy to social work practice. You may well ask what the law in particular has to do with you as a student of social work. The answer is simple: law and social policy affect practice at almost every turn. The law is the framework within which your practice must exist. If your practice were to operate outside of this framework, you would be acting illegally, so that cannot happen. Some laws are quite specific to your practice and in fact dictate what you may or may not do in any given circumstance. Other laws are quite circumspect and offer the opportunity for interpretation based upon professional judgements. Law is invariably aligned to policy, which does some of the interpreting for you and acts as a guide to practice as well as acting as the vehicle through which law can be enacted. There are also policies issued by agencies, having national policy and legislation as their guide, which will also affect you and your practice.

For a lively discussion of the law as it relates to social work in England and Wales (although many of the themes and issues are of relevance to your practice in Scotland) see Johns (2005).

The wider picture

This book is about social work with children, young people and their families in Scotland. It is, however, necessary to consider briefly both the European and the UK-wide context even though Scotland now has a devolved parliament.

The UK has a constitution, headed by the sovereign, which comprises many rules and procedures, both written (statute law and case law) and unwritten (for example, common law) which determine how the country is governed and how the different institutions within society relate to each other. This constitutional law derives its authority from convention, legislation and judicial decisions and from some other sources like the writings of some institutional writers such as Erskine, Hume and Stair, who are considered, certainly within Scots law, to be authoritative.

The Parliament of the UK is comprised of the sovereign, the House of Lords and the House of Commons. Between them they provide a government which generates legislation (laws) and regulations and policies to support these. The subsequent legal system(s) which have emerged, civil and criminal, serve to regulate our conduct by providing a framework of rules which aim to promote cooperation within society. By existing they set up a series of expectations against which society can determine (by and large) whether these expectations have been fulfilled (acting reasonably/legally) or not (acting unreasonably/illegally).

The criminal law provides sanctions or penalties against those who fail to comply with its terms. The standard required to prove that the criminal law has been broken is that of 'beyond reasonable doubt'. For example, in a situation where it is claimed that Mr Smith threw a stone through your window but he denied this, if several people had witnessed the event this type of evidence would probably be sufficient to prove beyond reasonable doubt that he was the culprit. In civil law, where a wrong is claimed to have been done by one against another (*delict*) the courts or a tribunal may arbitrate and the standard of proof is on the balance of probability, which means that the wrong was more or less likely to have been done as claimed. For example, Mrs Smith says that Mr Smith has been unreasonable in his behaviour during the course of their 10-year marriage and she wants a divorce. Mr Smith says that he hasn't and refuses to agree. In court, evidence might include Mrs Smith's friend who says that she has heard Mr Smith shouting at his wife and Mrs Smith's own testimony would also be taken into account, as would that of Mr Smith. This may be sufficient to prove, on the balance of probability, that Mr Smith has been unreasonable enough for the court to grant the divorce.

In social work with children, young people and their families, most (but not all) of the law you will refer to will be civil and will be dealt with either through the Sheriff or the High Courts or a tribunal. Where a child is harmed by a parent, redress would be through civil proceedings under the Children (Scotland) Act 1995 to afford protection, usually done through the children's hearing (a tribunal), but if it was thought that a criminal offence had been committed (sexual assault), then the criminal law would apply in relation to the alleged perpetrator and would be dealt with, at least initially, through the Sheriff Court. Thus, in complex situations like child sexual abuse, both strands of the law would operate.

The Scottish context

Civil and criminal laws operate UK-wide although there are differences in relation to their operation in Scotland as well as laws which are specific to Scotland. If you look at Figure 1.1 you will notice that the highest criminal court in Scotland is the High Court; there is no right of appeal to the House of Lords in Scotland in relation to criminal matters as there is in England and Wales. The names of the courts are also different. In England and Wales there are Magistrates' Courts, Crown Courts, the High Court and Courts of Appeal. In Scotland, there are District Courts, Sheriff Courts and the High Court. Judges are called Sheriffs in the Sheriff Courts. The High Court in Scotland acts as both a trial court and an appeal court and if it is felt that there has been a miscarriage of justice, there is recourse to the Scottish Criminal Cases Review Tribunal which has the power to refer cases back to the Appeal Court for consideration. There are also two different procedures in Scottish Courts: summary procedure, which means that the Sheriff will hear the case sitting alone; and solemn procedure, which means that the Sheriff or Judge will sit with a jury of 15 people. As the name implies, solemn procedure is used in more serious matters and in all appeals.

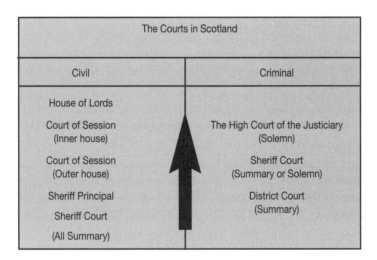

Figure 1.1 *The court structure in Scotland*

However, all of the laws of the UK have to be compatible with the European Convention on Human Rights and Fundamental Freedoms 1950 (ECHR) (incorporated into UK law by the Human Rights Act 1998 (UK)) as well as the United Nations Convention on the Rights of the Child (UNCRC) of which the UK is a signatory. Any domestic (Scottish or UK) law which does not subscribe to the principle of compatibility has to be reviewed or if it is applied it will become void.

Legislation and policy in Scotland after devolution

Scotland now has its own devolved parliament which came into existence following the granting of Royal Assent to the Scotland Act on 19 November 1998. Prior to this and as a direct result of the Act of Union of 1707, there had only been one Parliament in the UK, located at Westminster which legislated for England, Scotland, Northern Ireland and Wales, although the general affairs of Scotland (and Northern Ireland and Wales) have had some form of representation through their respective offices. In the case of Scotland this was the Scottish Office, headed up by a UK government minister with the title of Secretary of State for Scotland. During the latter part of the 20th century, however, concessions were made by the Westminster Parliament which granted limited powers to the other countries, and Regional Assemblies were formed in Northern Ireland and Wales, although their powers are not as clearly devolved as those in Scotland are now. This process of devolution, which is the delegation of central government powers to another body without relinquishing sovereignty, now means that the Scottish Parliament can control some of its own affairs. However, there are a number of matters which the Westminster Parliament and its UK government have reserved the right to continue to control. We therefore have *devolved* matters which can be controlled through the Scottish Parliament and the Scottish Executive, and *reserved* matters which are controlled from Westminster (see Tables 1.1 and 1.2).

Table 1.1 *The devolved powers of the Scottish Parliament*

• Education and Training	• Sports and Arts
• Local Government	• Farming and Fisheries
• Social Work	• Law and Home Affairs
• Agriculture	• Housing
• Statistics	• Police and Fire Services
• Health	• Planning
• Natural and Built Heritage	• Transport
• Environment	• Tourism and Economic Development
• Forestry and Fisheries	

Table 1.2 *The reserved matters of the Westminster Parliament*

- Foreign Affairs
- Defence and National Security
- Trade and Industry
- Social Security
- International Development
- Equal Opportunities
- Energy
- Broadcasting
- Constitutional Affairs
- Drug Misuse (aspects of)

- Economic Policy
- Common Markets
- Gambling
- Data Protection
- Abortion
- Human Fertilisation and Embryology
- Surrogacy Genetics
- Vivisection

ACTIVITY *1.1*

Look at the lists of devolved and reserved matters in Tables 1.1 and 1.2. Could any of them be moved and put into the other list? Think of the reasons that might lie behind the choices as they are at the moment.

Comment

You might have thought that devolved matters are all those which could be said to directly affect Scotland and have a more 'local' focus. For example, if you need a social work service in Scotland, you might rightly think that it makes sense for laws and policy about this to be made in Scotland (Edinburgh) rather than in England (London). Similarly, if you own a farm then the same reasoning might apply. But if this is the case, then should the same not apply to matters of trade and industry? There are a number of commentators who feel that this should be the case. For example, because there are substantial Scottish oil reserves, there is a view that control of these should be within Scotland and not in Westminster. It is also possible that these devolved powers and reserved matters may change. This tells us that social work, like almost every other aspect of social life, is influenced by politics. The Scottish Executive website is a good place to keep up to date on these matters (www.scotland.gov.uk).

The structure and function of the Scottish Parliament

The Scottish Parliament is responsible for forming committees and overseeing the work of the Scottish Executive, which is the government in Scotland for all devolved matters. The members of the Executive include the First Minister, the Lord Advocate, the Solicitor General and Members of the Scottish Parliament (MSPs) appointed as ministers. Thus, a Scottish minister is both a member of the Scottish Executive and the Scottish Parliament.

There are 129 MSPs of which 73 represent constituencies and 56 represent the eight regions. This representational arrangement is unique to Scotland. What it means is that each person in Scotland is represented by eight MSPs, one from their constituency and seven from within their particular region. MSPs can also be a Member of Parliament (an

MP) or a member of the European Parliament, having what is referred to as a *dual mandate*, although they can only hold a ministerial position in one or the other of the governments and they only get paid one salary.

The Scottish Executive has a number of departments, some of which have executive agencies attached to them which focus on specific areas and are accountable and report directly to Scottish ministers. The most relevant to children and young people are the Social Work Inspection Agency, which monitors the standards of social work services, and HM Inspectorate of Education, which inspects schools and other aspects of social care for children. These are referred to as 'arm's length' agencies which operate independently, although they are directly accountable to Scottish ministers.

The Executive also has a number of ministerial offices:

- Education and Young People
- Health and Community Care
- Office of the Deputy First Minister and Minister for Enterprise and Lifelong Learning
- Communities
- Tourism, Culture and Sport
- Finance and Public Service Reform
- Transport
- Justice
- Parliamentary Business
- Environment and Rural Development

It is largely through these ministerial offices that most of the major policy initiatives and directives emanate and it is worthwhile visiting the Scottish Executive website and following the links to look at these (www.scotland.gov.uk). These offices have a number of sections within them which focus on particular areas within the remit of the department. For example, the Office for Education and Young People has a Children and Young People's Group which concerns itself with the effective coordination of services for children and young people as well as working to ensure that all executive (i.e. governmental) policies work well together and are therefore integrated.

The political and policy process in Scotland

The Scottish Parliament does most of its work through the use of committees. These hold the Executive to account and may enquire into particular issues and report to Parliament. There are Standing or Mandatory Committees which exist permanently and focus upon issues like audit, procedures and other matters related to the business of Parliament as a whole. There are also a number of Subject Committees which Parliament has established with the aim of addressing specific policy issues within broad subject areas. These include Education, Health and Community Care, Social Inclusion, Housing and the Voluntary

Sector and Justice and Home Affairs, amongst others. These committees, be they mandatory or subject related, are able to form sub-committees which can be used to focus upon very specific issues from within the broader topic of inquiry. They can do this by seconding individuals or groups into their midst who may have expertise derived from social work practice, academia, business or some other sphere which it is felt can offer something to the matter under consideration. You may be called upon one day!

With regard to the creation of new or the amendment of existing laws (legislation), section 29 of the Scotland Act 1998 defines the parameters of the Scottish Parliament's power in this regard. Any legislation or amendments must be consistent with European Law and be compatible with the ECHR and the Human Rights Act 1998 (UK).

Where there is a need for new legislation or a need to amend existing laws, a Bill is introduced before Parliament, although a consultation exercise must be undertaken beforehand. A consultation must precede the introduction of any Bill and is the forum through which interested parties may comment and respond to the proposals, including you. Consultations can be seen at: www.scotland.gov.uk/views/consult.asp

There are four main types of Bill:

- Executive Bills are those drafted and introduced by the Scottish Executive. These Bills have to be accompanied by a Financial Memorandum and a Ministerial Statement explaining the rationale for the Bill, its objectives and its likely (hoped for) impact. Of note is the notion of developing Child Impact Statements which are being considered for use in relation to all legislative and policy initiatives to make explicit the likely impact upon children (in general) of any initiative, irrespective of its main focus. So, for example, there may be a Bill introduced relating to fish quotas in the North Sea. The Child Impact Statement may well assess the impact upon children to be negligible (probably correctly). However, a Bill introduced with the intention of regulating childminding arrangements would have a major impact upon children and the possible effects would need to be clearly articulated in order that ministers and the public (through consultations) can respond in order to influence such matters through the democratic process.

- Members Bills are introduced by any MSP who is not a member of the Scottish Executive.

- Committee Bills are introduced by committees. These Bills may arise following the deliberations of a committee into a particular issue.

- Private Bills are introduced by an individual or an organisation.

There is also a procedure known as a *Sewel Motion* whereby the Scottish Parliament can adopt a piece of Westminster legislation and apply it to Scotland. This avoids the need to duplicate activity. A recent example would be use of a Sewel Motion to aspects of the Adoption and Children Act 2002, which was originally designed to extend only to England and Wales.

The political process and the policy-making process are interconnected. It is through these processes that laws and policy become real and have an impact upon people's lives. But people's lives and experiences and the experiences of practitioners also affect these processes. Figure 1.2 shows how this happens in general terms. However, many laws are quite circumspect with regard to particular issues offering broad scope for subsequent interpretation by the courts (via *case law* and *precedent*) and other tribunals, and legislation is invariably accompanied by Regulations and Guidance. For example, the Children (S) Act 1995 is accompanied by four volumes of Regulations and Guidance (Scottish Office 1997a, b, c, d).

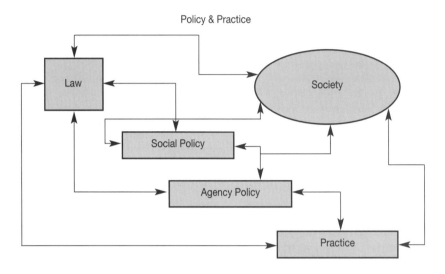

Figure 1.2 *The relationship between law, policy, practice and people*

We shall now turn to a detailed consideration of the development of legislation and policy in Scotland. You will see how the influence of history, politics, policy initiatives, practice developments and people's lives all merge to create the practice framework we have today. You will also see that these issues are socially constructed and reflect society at any given time (James and Prout 2003).

The development of social policy and social work in Scotland

ACTIVITY 1.2

Whilst reading this section, try to identify any themes which emerge. For example, when do themes like the 'welfare principle' and 'early intervention' first appear and how are they articulated? Do they disappear only to reappear later on? See Tisdall and Kay (1997) and Murphy (1992).

The law and social policy

It is important to appreciate the relevance and significance of social policy and how it has developed and evolved over time. This is important too in allowing you to appreciate how

the social work profession has emerged within the context of social policy, both historically and contemporaneously.

Social policies may well develop as a result of the passing of certain pieces of legislation or
as a result of social movements and trends. The law may well be written or rewritten to
reflect such trends and pressures. Everything relates to everything else and you might even
say that there is a *symbiosis* in evidence. You might want to look at Figure 1.2 again to
remind yourself of these interrelationships. In the area of child care social work, the Children
(S) Act 1995 is a good example of changes arising as a result of trends and pressures.

WHAT IS SOCIAL POLICY?

*Social policy is a discrete academic discipline in its own right as well as a way of referring
to 'the activity of policy-making to promote well-being' (Alcock 2003, p3). Central to any
consideration of social policy is the issue of state (public) involvement in private life. Social
policies, much like defence policies or economic policies, affect everyone at some level or
another. When we study social policy we are concerned with understanding the impact of
these public policies and how they contribute to, or detract from, the well-being or welfare of individuals and/or groups in society.*

Studying the development of policy allows you to appreciate the full context of current
policy initiatives; there is much to be found in historical documentation which can be
quite revealing. There are also a number of statutes (laws) which are still in force, despite
them being made a long time ago. There are also a number of statutes which have been
partially repealed. What this means is that newer legislation has been enacted which has
replaced some of an earlier enactment, but not all. A good example would be the partial
repeal of the Social Work (S) Act 1968 by the Children (S) Act 1995. Each new enactment
states which aspects of which earlier statute it is repealing. The details can usually be
found at the end of the new statute as 'Extent, Short Title, Minor and Consequential
Amendments, Repeals and Commencement'.

In order to illustrate some of these points, it might be worthwhile considering where the
welfare principle (s.16 Children (S) Act 1995) came from. It was in fact first mentioned in
the Children and Young Persons (S) Act 1932 (s.16). Thus, principles we readily identify
with today have clear antecedents.

Legislation and policy for children, young people and their families in Scotland

The Children Act (UK) 1908 is generally regarded as the first 'Children's Charter' because
of its wide-ranging impact and its concern for the rights of children. This Act abolished the
death sentence for children and put restrictions upon why, when and for how long children could be imprisoned. This may appear somewhat shocking but this is a good example
of how attitudes are a product of their time and how they can change. The 1908 (UK) Act
also established the notion of separate Juvenile Courts rather than having children appearing in adult courts with all its pomp and ceremony, which can be very intimidating, even

to the most experienced practitioner. This began to pave the way for what might be regarded as a more enlightened attitude to children and young people, recognising that in many instances they were victims rather than the guilty.

Essentially, the 1908 Act laid the foundations for child protection under the law and it made specific reference to public authorities having to act in a way which aimed to prevent cruelty and neglect to children and young people, although in practise this was often achieved by simply removing them from their homes.

During the inter-war years, there were a number of committees set up which reported upon a range of issues relating to the treatment and protection of children which were subsequently encapsulated in the Children and Young Persons (S) Act 1937. This Act raised the age of criminal responsibility from 7 to 8 years and defined a *child* as being someone under the age of 14 years, whilst a *young person* was someone between 14 and 17 years. These issues are of interest in allowing us to get a glimpse of changing conceptions of childhood throughout recent history. The definitions (because there are more than one) of a child in Scotland today are to be found in section 93(2)a) and b) of the 1995 Act. The 1937 (S) Act also developed the idea from the 1908 (UK) Act of separating children and young people from the court system, and developed separate panels of Justices; these could be said to be the forerunners of the Children's Panels we have today, although the Kilbrandon Committee had much to do with this.

Of great significance was section 49 (s.49) of the 1937 (S) Act. This referred to courts/others having regard to the welfare of the child. This heralded the end of an era where punishment was deemed to be the only way to deal with children who offended, irrespective of age and circumstance. The welfare principle was born. All of these measures represented a significant shift towards recognising that the state and its individual members had responsibilities towards and in respect of children, although the tendency of adults to exercise rights over children still dominated society at that time. The 1937 Act remained the mainstay of social work practice, especially with regard to juvenile justice, until the implementation of the Social Work (S) Act 1968.

In terms of the impact of this legislation upon social work practice, children who were felt to have been deprived of a normal home life and upbringing were generally removed from home. They were either sent to an approved school or were 'boarded out' (early foster care). In terms of the broader social context at this time, removal was felt to be justifiable by reference to the fact that housing was generally of a poor standard. The infrastructure to support children remaining at home did not really exist. Policy and practice can be seen to be intimately connected with structural factors (housing, public health, etc.). It was also the case that the organisational arrangements for the public care of children were still rather basic and the number of people opting to work in this field was relatively small.

These arrangements were felt to work reasonably well, however, although this has to be seen in context. At this time in history, although attitudes towards children were beginning to change, issues such as the impact upon the child of being removed from home did not merit much consideration. The view was one which sought to deprive 'feckless' parents of the opportunity to parent rather than to consider whether the solution might be worse than the problem. The children were offered a substitute home (often in rural/crofting areas) which provided all that their real home appeared not to. As far as most people were concerned at that time, the removal of the child from the poor home removed the problem, and *ergo*, everyone was happy. However, things were about to change.

The impact of the war years

In the immediate post-war years of the 1940s, the government had to reconsider its position in relation to children and young people. The effects of the evacuation of large numbers of children during the war years had made people realise just how bad conditions were for many in the cities. Those evacuated to 'safe havens' were sometimes greeted with incredulity by their carers who had not appreciated the full significance of poor housing, the effects of poverty and, one might argue, that of poor parenting. There was also concern over what to do about the large numbers of children who, for a variety of reasons, were unable to return home at the end of the war.

Concern was growing over the care of children in public care and the case of Denis O'Neill (Home Office 1945) who died whilst in 'foster care' in England added impetus to the calls for a major review of child care provision. Concerns were also growing over the way in which child care services were being delivered. The work of people like Bowlby (1997) and Winnicott (1958) on the importance of attachments, plus the actions of a number of powerful people and the publication of a pamphlet by Lady Allen, entitled *Whose children?* (1945) all served to focus attention upon the importance of listening to the child in relation to their experiences.

The Curtis Committee (E & W) (1946, Cmnd 6922) and the Clyde Committee on Child Care in Scotland (1946, Cmnd 6911) were set up independently in the wake of the inquiry into the death of Denis O'Neill amidst growing concerns about public child care provision. Both paved the way for the Children Act 1948 (UK). Responsibility for services to children rested with Children's Departments and 'Boarding Out' (foster care) was promoted. The primary focus was to support those children already deprived of a normal home life and who had been placed in substitute care. One criticism of the Clyde Committee who supported this scheme was the practice of sending city children to rural areas, which caused them considerable distress. People were now beginning to realise that children had feelings. And, relative to our views of today where we are more aware of the issues of loss, change and transitions, the penny was beginning to drop.

Child abuse and neglect as a social issue

Child abuse and neglect have not always been recognised in the way they are today. In the post-war years child abuse and neglect had not yet become embedded within the national psyche; this had to wait for the findings of Kempe et al. (1962) and others to highlight the phenomenon for what it was. However, the 1948 Act had not been in force for long before it was realised that the practice focus of targeting resources towards those youngsters already in public care was only addressing part of the problem, i.e. that of children who had already been the victims of abuse and neglect. What about those children who were still at home and on the receiving end of poor parenting and poor living conditions? It had been suggested during the committee stage of the (then) Children's Bill that an amendment ought to be added which placed a duty on local authorities to support the parents of (neglected) children; unfortunately this was rejected and this duty had to wait a while longer before making an appearance. But in an attempt to be seen to respond constructively, the government of the day issued circulars directing local authorities to 'keep in mind' the need to do all they could to protect those children still at home from being abused and neglected. There were no further statutory measures at this time; rather there were a range of administrative measures brought to bear on overstretched agencies (Murphy 1992).

ACTIVITY **1.3**

Can you identify any themes which may be emerging? What do you think was being done about the effect of structural issues (e.g. poor housing and poverty)? See Murphy (1992) and Fraser (2003) for a very good (UK) overview.

The child in context

At this time we can see more attention being given to the need to prevent abuse and neglect before it reached the stage where youngsters had to be removed. Whether this was a genuine response by the government intending to reduce misery, or a response to overstretched and recently criticised 'boarding-out' schemes it is difficult to say. However, different sorts of (awkward) questions were now being asked about the condition of our children, not just in terms of their physical well-being, but also about their emotional well-being.

More attention was being given to considering the child in his/her wider context. What was happening at home? What was happening at school? What did the child enjoy doing? These early beginnings foreshadow the *ecological approach*, commonly taken today (Bronfenbrenner 1979; Jack 2000). The term 'problem family' was now being used and officials were beginning to ask why it might be that certain families seemed to be unable to reach and/or maintain minimum standards despite input from the Children's Departments. These Departments began to utilise a range of additional services to assist them in delivering services. These included the NSPCC and the Family Service Units (E & W) which adopted a more holistic and, some would say, therapeutic approach. In Scotland similar developments took place, notably in Dundee where a training home was opened for mothers with their youngsters. These residential training homes were often an alternative to prison for many mothers (which raises some very interesting issues about the role (or not) of fathers in terms of child welfare/parenting, many of which are still evident today) and other arrangements included semi-staffed/supported residences which offered a range of services to assist in the parenting task. In many ways, these could be seen as the forerunners of our parent education programmes in family centres.

In terms of early intervention, its first real appearance within officialdom can be seen in a report from 1963 which called for increased practical help for families and better training for workers to aid the early identification of problems (McBoyle 1963). The title of this report has, for me, a certain irony: *Working together: problem families*. The 'working together' theme has been around for a long time and is a familiar mantra today. Clearly, this approach was being seen as the way forward with due recognition being given to the interrelated nature of many of the difficulties encountered by families (Murphy 1992).

Working together, prevention and early intervention: the beginnings of integration

These thematic developments relating to prevention, early identification and practical help took shape in Scotland through the deliberations of the Committee on the Prevention of Neglect of Children (The McBoyle Committee) between 1961 and 1963 (Cmnd 1966). Their remit was to consider whether local authorities should have additional powers to prevent children suffering through neglect in their own homes. The committee argued that a major weakness of the current arrangements related to barriers to communication and an absence of sufficiently trained workers, all compounded by poor coordination. The main recommendations referred to the granting of additional powers (not duties) to local authorities to allow them to provide 'comprehensive services' for the prevention of neglect which should, of necessity, include the giving of practical help, either in kind or in cash, the development of family advice centres and the provision of training centres for families. These recommendations were central to the provisions of the Children and Young Persons Act 1963 (UK), especially section 1, whose main aim was to promote the welfare of the child by diminishing the need to receive them into or keep them in care. The 1963 Act placed a new duty upon local authorities to undertake preventative work with children and their families.

The practice of social casework (Biestek 1961) began to emerge, which was seen as the best way to provide services. This arrangement involved workers undertaking assessments and providing assistance designed to help people resolve their difficulties. Central to this approach was the relationship that developed between the worker and the family. Family-aides were also used along with specialist home-helps and 'foster mothers' for day-care provision. There was an increased emphasis upon sharing information and cooperation between authorities, at least relative to how things had been done before. The expectations upon Children's Departments increased dramatically because people were now beginning to realise that families and children in need often required the services of a number of workers simultaneously.

Juvenile delinquency

In the 1950s and 1960s, juvenile delinquency had been a major social issue and courts had been flooded with referrals. In England and Wales the Ingleby Committee had formed to respond to the phenomena there. In Scotland, the Kilbrandon Committee was formed in 1961 and reported in 1964 (Cmnd 2306) on its remit to consider the provisions of the law in Scotland in relation to juvenile delinquents and those in need of care and protection.

Kilbrandon took a rather radical approach for the time by emphasising the central importance of the needs of the child within any given situation and the relevance to the child's situation of the failure of the upbringing (parenting) process. Chapter 2 looks at this in more detail.

Scotland was thus leading the way with regards to children and young people and the issue of delinquency, making important distinctions between *needs* and *deeds*. However, implementation of the report's recommendations came later following upheavals relating to the reorganisation of social services in Scotland where, like other areas of the UK, services were generally felt to be disorganised, repetitive and inefficient. These views concerning the state of social services at the time stemmed from the increasing recognition that work with vulnerable families often involved contact with a range of personnel, and the way in which services were being organised and delivered left a lot to be desired. With the ethos of prevention clearly in the frame, questions were being asked as to how the delivery of services might be made more meaningful.

The implementation of the recommendations of Kilbrandon had to wait until the introduction of the Social Work (S) Act 1968. This significant piece of legislation did a number of things with, to and for social work. It brought together all existing social work services within one framework, placing the responsibility for the provision of all social work services within local authority social work departments, including probation services (now Criminal Justice Services). The Act also introduced a specific duty upon local authorities to 'promote social welfare by making available advice, guidance and assistance on such a scale as may be appropriate for their area' (s.12(1)). Section 12 of the 1968 Act (still in force and amended by the NHS and Community Care Act 1990 (UK)) meant that local authorities now had to do more than respond to need; they had to go and look for it, categorise it and respond to it before it became a problem. This new duty also extended beyond individuals so that working with groups of people and communities to prevent difficulties emerging was now seen as a legitimate and a necessary activity.

SECTION 12

Section 12(1) of the Social Work (S) Act 1968 states that:

> *It shall be the duty of every local authority to promote social welfare by making available advice, guidance and assistance on such a scale as may be appropriate for their area, and in that behalf to make arrangements and to provide or secure the provision of such facilities (including the provision or arranging for the provision of residential and other establishments) as they may consider suitable and adequate, and such assistance may be given to, or in respect of, the persons specified in the next following subsection in kind or in cash, subject to subsections (3) and (4) of this section.*

Reproduced under the terms of Crown Copyright Policy Guidance Issued by HMSO.

Protection or prevention?

The 1968 Act resulted in a clear divergence from the rest of the UK. The Scottish child care system had a strong welfare basis for the delivery of its services, whilst in England and Wales there remained a strong justice-based approach. There were tensions in existence across the UK, but especially in England and Wales, and these were perhaps exemplified by the passing of the Children Act 1975 (UK) which many saw as representing the pinnacle of state intervention into family life. Whilst the Act made it clear that the welfare of the child was to be the first consideration, there was a clear shift towards adopting a more judicially based approach to achieve this. This had the effect of marginalising the rights of both parents and children and a 'save and rescue' approach seemed to develop.

Lorraine Fox-Harding (1997) summarises four value perspectives which have, to a greater or lesser extent, permeated child care policy and practice at different periods of time. I think that there are elements of these different positions evident most of the time, although aspects of some are more dominant than others. These positions can be summarised as follows:

1. *Laissez-faire and patriarchy*: this perspective has deep historical roots and is often associated with the 19th century and industrialisation. This view would hold that the power in and of the family should not be disturbed or encroached upon except in extreme circumstances. The role for the state is seen as being minimal.

2. *State paternalism and child protection*: this perspective can be seen to emerge with the growth of welfare provision *per se* in the late 19th/early 20th centuries. State intervention in order to care for and protect children is legitimated. The actions of the state may, however, be seen as authoritarian and the issue of the importance of biological bonds minimised. To this extent, the rights of parents are minimised and the child's welfare is paramount.

3. *The modern defence of the birth family and parents' rights*: this view is associated with the expansion of welfare provision. State intervention is legitimate, but its form is distinct from *laissez-faire* and is not paternalistic in that it is supportive, promoting the preservation of the family unit. Structural factors are deemed to be important variables to be taken into account in relation to the reasons for and the nature of interventions.

4. *Children's rights and child liberation*: this advocates for the child to be seen as the subject, as an independent person, with rights of their own.

(Fox-Harding 1997, p9)

All of these perspectives can be seen to have some place within the broad historical context of child care policy and practice. All of them have weak and strong forms and in that regard exist on a continuum. It is tempting to see aspects of all of these perspectives having some relevance at any given time and if we look at legislation and policy closely it is possible to see this.

A number of high-profile events in the UK in the 1980s and early 1990s made people sit up and think about what was happening in relation to social work with children, young people and their families. We shall look at four which will give you an understanding of the complexities, confusion and conflict evident during this time.

Each of the situations referred to in the Research Summary on page 18 speaks to the dilemmas faced by social workers and their managers in terms of safeguarding and promoting the welfare of children whilst trying to respect the family and do things in the best way possible within the constraints of finite resources. In Jasmine's situation, workers had too much regard for the parents' views and too little for hers; in Cleveland and Orkney, the reverse could be said to be true. In Fife, attempts to play things 'by the book' left professionals feeling de-skilled, unsure as to their own competence and afraid to challenge the views of managers even when they knew they were right.

Concern, confusion and conflict in child care

The tragic death of Jasmine Beckford brought to the public's attention the failings of social work services who appeared to have done nothing to prevent this despite social workers visiting the home and having contact with the family. The report, A child in trust *(Blom-Cooper 1985) was highly critical of the way social workers appeared to focus upon the family, effectively rendering Jasmine invisible. There was also criticism of the view practitioners appeared to have of 'natural love', the implication of this being that no harm would befall children because a parent would instinctively protect them. This had the effect of blinkering professionals to what was really going on.*

The events in Cleveland in 1987 saw all professionals involved in child protection work severely criticised for removing children thought to have been sexually abused. Social work found itself in a double-bind; criticised when they did not intervene appropriately (as in the case of Jasmine Beckford), and condemned for removing children they believed were being sexually abused (as in Cleveland). In all of these situations, a balance had to be struck between respecting the autonomy and privacy of the family and protecting children.

In early 1991, events on the Orkney Islands were to send shock waves through the whole of the UK. Here, a number of children suspected of being the victims of organised sexual abuse were removed from their families. This situation raised a number of issues about the whole practice of child protection work; public outcry regarding the actions of the social work teams and other professionals and agencies was vociferous and condemnation loud and clear. The subsequent report into these events (the Clyde Report 1992) makes interesting reading. This report paved the way for a greater role for the courts in welfare decisions concerning children and their families. A number of safeguards were put in place which essentially limited the power of social work departments and their administrative powers as well as a number of recommendations (194 in total) concerning the conduct of agencies in respect of working together more cooperatively (not a new theme). These events signalled a shift with regard to the relationships that existed not only between the family and the state, but between the state and the courts. However, further events were about to unfold in Scotland which would lead to the White Paper, Proposals for child care policy and law *(1993), which was essentially the blueprint for the Children (S) Act 1995.*

In 1992 events in Fife led to a report being published concerning the rigid implementation of policy in that area which compromised good child care practice. Because of tensions between a number of agencies in the area involved in child care and protection work, Fife social work managers issued a series of policy documents which, superficially, were seen as the embodiment of good child care practice. The problems emerged when they were implemented, as managers insisted that they be implemented literally. The welfare discretion and professional judgement of social workers was effectively removed. The result was that the numbers of children who were received into the care of the local authority dropped significantly; in and of itself that may be seen as no bad thing, but what was clear was that many of these children were in need of care and protection, but did not receive it because of strict managerial policies which effectively forbade social workers from doing their jobs.

The report into the practices in Fife was followed by a review of the role and function of the Reporter to the Children's Panel (1992) and inquiries into the state of residential child care in Scotland (*Caring for the future* and *Another kind of home* (The Skinner Report) (both 1992).

The year 1993 saw the report of the Review of Adoption Law alongside the Report on Family Law (No. 135) (SLC1992). These led to the production of the White Paper, *Scotland's children: proposals for child care policy and law* (Social Work Services Group 1993) and took the view that the 'default position' for children should be for them to be with their families where this was seen to be in their interests. This arrangement should only be interrupted on 'formally stated grounds' with orders to protect children requested on the basis that they were at risk of significant harm, and not on the basis that the child's welfare simply required it. As a result, considerable grounds had to be established before a Child Protection Order (CPO) could be granted, thereby moving the balance away from social work's welfare discretion towards greater judicial control. Some commentators felt that the whole arena of child protection work was being siphoned away from the children's hearing and placed within the domain of the court, in many respects appearing to run counter to the ethos of the children's hearing system. The distinction between welfare (the remit of the children's hearing) and justice (the remit of the court) was seen by some to be being eroded.

Implementation of the Children (S) Act 1995 began on 1 April 1997 and one of its major claims is that this one piece of legislation considers the position of children within the spheres of public and private law, as well as maintaining its emphasis upon the rights of the child and the responsibilities of parents towards them. These and other related measures could be seen as a compromise which attempts to balance the issue of the welfare of the child with the oversight of due process offered by the courts.

The contemporary scene

The development of policy and practice in Scotland has a long and interesting history. The previous sections have detailed how social work practice has evolved within a number of different statutory frameworks over a period of time. The history lesson is important in helping you to understand why things are the way they are today.

The Children (S) Act 1995 represents the central piece of the child care platform upon and within which contemporary child care practice operates. There are a number of other important statutes which relate to child care as well as a number of very significant policy initiatives which have emerged over the past few years. Table 1.3 lists some of the main legislative components of the current child care scene. Others will be referred to in the appropriate chapters.

Table 1.3 *Primary legislation*

Primary legislation

- Social Work (S) Act 1968
- Adoption (S) Act 1978
- Education (S) Act 1980
- Matrimonial Homes (Family Protection) (S) Act 1981
- Disabled Persons (Services, Consultation and Representation) Act 1986
- Law Reform (Parent and Child) (S) Act 1986
- Age of Legal Capacity (S) Act 1991
- **Children (Scotland) Act 1995**
- Human Rights Act 1998 (UK)
- Regulation of Care (S) Act 2001
- Adoption and Children Act 2002 (UK)
- Commissioner for Children and Young People (S) Act 2002
- Community Care and Health (S) Act 2002
- Criminal Justice (S) Act 2003
- Mental Health (Care and Treatment) (S) Act 2003
- Protection of Children (S) Act 2003
- Anti-Social Behaviour etc. (S) Act 2004
- Education (Additional Support for Learning) (S) Act 2004

Another area to be aware of is that relating to Rules, Regulations and Guidance, often referred to as *subordinate* or *secondary* legislation. The function of this type of legislation is to implement and put into operation *primary* legislation. Table 1.4 lists the main sources of rules, regulations and guidance.

Table 1.4 *Secondary legislation, regulations and guidance*

- Arrangements to Look After Children (S) Regulations (1996)
- Children's Hearings (S) Rules (1996)
- Fostering of Children (S) Regulations (1996)
- Secure Accommodation (S) Regulations 1996
- Act of Sederunt (Child Care and Maintenance Rules) (1997)
- Children (S) Act Regulations and Guidance (Vols 1–4) (1997)
- Supporting Young People Leaving Care in Scotland Regulations (2004)

These two sets of laws are central to the current operation of child care practice in Scotland. In addition, there are a range of policy initiatives of which it is important for you to be aware. These are listed in Table 1.5.

Table 1.5 *Current policy initiatives*

- Child Protection: A Shared Responsibility (1998)
- New Community Schools (1998)
- Sure Start (1998)
- Modernising Government (1999)
- Social Inclusion Strategy (1999)
- Social Justice: A Scotland Where Everyone Matters (1999)
- Community Care: A Joint Future (2000)
- Towards a Healthier Scotland (2000)
- Care Commission (2001)
- Changing Children's Services Fund (2001)
- For Scotland's Children: Better Integrated Children's Services (2001)
- National Care Standards (2001)
- Promoting Children's Mental health within Early Years and School Settings (2001)
- Child Protection Reform Programme (2002)
- 'It's Everyone's Job to Make Sure I'm Alright' : Report of the Child Protection Audit and Review (2002)
- Vulnerable Witnesses Programme (2002)

- Youth Justice Strategy (2002)
- Getting it Right for Every Child: A Review of the Children's Hearing System (2003)
- Getting Our Priorities Right (2003)
- Integrated Strategy for Early Years (2003)
- Making It Work for Scotland's Children: Report of the Child Health Support Group (2003)
- Single Shared Assessments (2003)
- Framework for Standards in Child Protection (2004)
- Growing Support: A Review of Services for Vulnerable Families (2004)
- National Framework for Promoting Positive Mental Health and Well-Being (2004)
- 21C Social Work: Review of Social Work (2004)

The current legislative and policy context is one which has evolved over time. Where things are now is as a result of where we have been, for better or for worse. It is possible to see themes developing as a result of changes in society and shifts in attitudes towards the way we view the nature of childhood, the family and society as a whole. Social phenomena, such as increases in youth offending, are not new; look back at the section on p 15 under 'Juvenile delinquency.' Today's Youth Justice Initiative is another attempt to deal with such phenomena with, we hope, enlightened attitudes based upon experience.

Events within society which require a collective response through the development of social policies are what Tables 1.3 to 1.5 refer to. The Scottish Executive has as its aim the development of public services which are integrated ('seamless') and able to respond to need effectively. In terms of planning, there are now Integrated Children's Services Plans (see s.19 of the 1995 Act) which aim to ensure that all local authorities plan services in a coordinated way. These plans must involve other service delivery agents: education departments, NHS Boards, other departments within social work, housing services and voluntary organisations. The frameworks which are now in evidence do connect to each other and support practice in a more integrated way. The chapters which follow will illustrate this in some detail, but the main themes to bear in mind at this point in relation to the legal and policy context are: rights; planning; integration; funding; and information sharing. This last point has relevance far in excess of its presence on the page. The sharing of information is crucial in ensuring that children, young people and their families receive services which are responsive to their needs, flexible, equitable and useful to them. Inter-agency collaboration is central to this and can only be achieved by effective and efficient information sharing which respects people's rights.

C H A P T E R   S U M M A R Y

In Chapter 1 we have considered the historical development of law, (social) policy and practice as it relates to children, young people and their families in Scotland. We have looked at the European, UK-wide and Scottish contexts in order to appreciate how the influence of *supra-state* legislation affects *domestic* legislation. You have also seen how the current legislative and policy framework emphasises *integration* and how these frameworks facilitate inter-agency collaboration.

FURTHER READING

Alcock, **P**, **Erskine**, **A** and **May**, **M** (2003) *The student's companion to social policy (2nd edition).* Oxford: Blackwell.

Baillie, **D**, **Cameron**, **C**, **Cull**, **L-A**, **Roche**, **J** and **West**, **J** (eds) (2003) *Social work and the law in Scotland.* Basingstoke: Palgrave Macmillan/Open University.

McNorrie, **K McK** (1998) *The Children (Scotland) Act 1995 (2nd edition).* Greens Annotated Acts. Edinburgh: W. Green & Son.

Tisdall, **E** and **Kay M** (1997) *The Children (Scotland) Act 1995: developing policy and law for Scotland's children.* Edinburgh: Children in Scotland/The Stationery Office.

WEBSITES

www.scotland.gov.uk

www.scottish.parliament.uk

www.childpolicy.org.uk

Chapter 2

The children's hearing system and youth justice

A C H I E V I N G   A   S O C I A L   W O R K   D E G R E E

This chapter will help you to meet the following Scottish Standards in Social Work Education (SiSWE) (Scottish Executive 2003a: available at www.scotland.gov.uk/library5/social/ffsw.pdf).

Key Role 1: Prepare for, and work with, individuals, families, carers, groups and communities to assess their needs and circumstances.

1:1 Preparing for social work contact and involvement.

1:2 Working with individuals, families, carers, groups and communities so they can make informed decisions.

1:3 Assessing needs and options in order to recommend a course of action.

Key Role 4: Demonstrate professional competence in social work practice.

4:1 Evaluating and using up-to-date knowledge of, and research into, social work practice.

4:2 Working within agreed standards of social work practice.

4:3 Understanding and managing complex ethical issues, dilemmas and conflicts.

4:4 Promoting best social work practice, adapting positively to change.

Key Role 6: Support individuals to represent and manage their needs, views and circumstances.

6:1 Representing, in partnership with, and on behalf of, individuals, families, carers, groups and communities to help them achieve and maintain greater independence.

Introduction

The children's hearing system (CHS) is unique to Scotland. One of its basic tenets is that the needs of the child come first, whether they are the offender or have been offended against. All children are dealt with by the same system in a manner which takes account of all their circumstances and does not involve the courts, except in certain circumstances. This is a very different arrangement from that which exists in other parts of the UK (Johns 2005).

In this chapter, we will look at how the children's hearing system evolved, how it is structured, who it involves, how it works, what it can do and how it can do it. In your work with children, young people and their families it is almost inevitable that you will come into contact with the CHS in some way, shape or form, so you do need to have a working knowledge of it.

This chapter will focus upon the broad arrangements of the CHS and will consider its location within the spectrum of services designed to respond to children in need of care and protection and those who are offending and who may therefore require a response which equates more closely with the requirements for (criminal) justice, because as Whyte (2004), citing Adler (1985, p2), notes:

> *...it is perhaps misguided to try to attempt to squeeze the facts of childhood into a unified theory. In many jurisdictions youth justice systems run in parallel and even conflict with social work and educational systems, and have tended to be evaluated against ideal types of welfare or justice as if the two were incompatible (p396).*

In Scotland, the CHS operates dualistically and considers the offender and those offended against, recognising that the needs of both are often the same. In some ways the CHS appears to achieve a level of compatibility which Adler (1985, p2), cited in Whyte (*ibid*), suggests is an ideal:

> *Any system dealing with young people who offend needs to be sufficiently flexible to accommodate conflicting theories to achieve justice for children, instead of denying the conflicts of childhood to achieve a coherent philosophy.*

The CHS, like any other system, has its strengths and weaknesses and it is important that these be acknowledged. One area where the CHS has some difficulty is in dealing with serious and persistent offenders (Audit Scotland 2002). The Scottish Executive has responded to these matters (Scottish Executive 2000) and produced a 10-point action plan with a focus on reducing youth crime (Scottish Executive 2002a) involving a number of measures and initiatives which attempt to complement and support the role of the CHS. There is also an overarching review of children's services being undertaken which includes a review of the CHS as part of this (Scottish Executive 2005a).

The origins of the children's hearing system

The CHS as we know it today has a lengthy history and its evolution can be traced back to concerns over the way in which children who had committed offences were treated, including the growing realisation that despite the fact that a child had offended, they needed to be helped rather than punished.

The origins of one of the principles epitomised by the CHS, that children and young people need to be treated separately and differently from adults, can be traced back to the Children Act 1908 (UK). It was this piece of legislation which began the process of developing specific provision for dealing with children (7 years and above at the time) and young people (up to the age of 17 years at that time) who had committed offences. A report from the Morton Committee (1928) recommended that special Juvenile Courts be established, headed up by a Justice of the Peace (JP) with special knowledge and experience of children. These Juvenile Courts were designed to reduce some of the pomp and ceremony associated with adult courts and minimise the sense of intimidation encountered as a result of the surroundings and proceedings. The recommendations of the Morton Committee were incorporated into the Children and Young Persons (S) Act 1932, which created separate panels of Justices who would deal with children referred to them rather than to the adult courts (s.1) and it also increased the minimum age of criminal responsibility from 7 to 8 years of age, where it remains to this day in Scotland. These panels also had a 'non-criminal' function bestowed upon them in recognition of the fact that some children were in need of 'care and protection'.

Despite their limitations, these panels were very clearly the forerunners of the children's panels we have today, even though they were still part of the mainstream court system. The Children and Young Person's (S) Act 1937 (which added to the provisions of the earlier Act of 1932) was the mainstay of juvenile justice and child welfare provision until the implementation of the Social Work (S) Act 1968. In practise, however, these arrangements were implemented rather inconsistently and the whole issue of how to deal appropriately and effectively with children and young people continued to present itself as a challenge.

Juvenile delinquency and children in need of care and protection

In the 1950s and 1960s, juvenile delinquency was seen as a major social problem. In England and Wales the Ingleby Committee had been formed to respond to the issue, and in Scotland the Kilbrandon Committee was formed in 1961 with its remit:

> to consider the provisions of the law in Scotland relating to the treatment of juvenile delinquents and juveniles in need of care and protection or beyond parental control and, in particular, the constitution, powers and procedure of the courts dealing with such juveniles, and to report.
>
> (Scottish Home and Health Department and Scottish Education Department (Cmnd 2306: 1964, p7).

The establishment of the Kilbrandon Committee reflected the concerns that children were being treated inconsistently in different types of courts despite the provisions of the 1937 Act and that these practices were developing more in response to local issues rather than being based upon a set of sound and clearly articulated principles accepted and implemented across the board.

Kilbrandon took a rather radical approach for the time by emphasising the central importance of the needs of the child within any given situation and the relevance to them of the 'failure' of the upbringing (parenting) process. The committee adopted an educational approach which aimed to harness and build upon the 'natural influences' within the child's life. The most obvious of these was the family and it was felt that measures to treat the child should involve working with the whole family.

In terms of its recommendations, Kilbrandon sought to remove all cases involving children and young people from the mainstream court system and transfer the responsibility for dealing with them to newly established Juvenile Panels. Issues relating to guilt and/or innocence would still be left to the courts, whilst decisions relating to the welfare of the child would now rest with the panels, and standards of proof in civil law were to be applied. All referrals were to be centralised through a Reporter to the Panel in order that coordination could be maximised and four main categories were established:

- referrals in relation to children and young people who offended;

- referrals in relation to those who were offended against (in need of care and/or protection);

- referrals in relation to those who were beyond control;
- referrals in relation to those who were not attending school.

In all of these categories the welfare principle was seen as being paramount to the remit and functioning of the panels. The welfare principle currently articulated in section 16(1) of the Children (S) Act 1995 first appeared in the 1932 Act (which was also s.16) and was the first recognition, in statute, of the need for courts and other bodies to look beyond the immediately presenting situation and consider what the child needed in order to improve the overall situation and, crucially, to promote their welfare. In doing this, the committee recognised the need for a full assessment before matters were brought before the panel, where a full and frank discussion would take place. The committee also had to consider those children and young people who had not themselves offended but had been offended against and were therefore in need of care and protection.

ACTIVITY **2.1**

Take a look at section 6 of the Children and Young Persons (S) Act 1932, section 65 of the Children and Young Persons (S) Act 1937, section 32 of the Social Work (S) Act 1968 and section 52 of the Children (S) Act 1995.

Make a note of the categories of referral that exist in each of them. Are there more now? If so, why do you think this is?

These statutes will be in your library.

Comment

You might have noticed strong similarities in the way the grounds of referral are framed and how they have evolved over time. These developments reflect changes in attitudes, opinions and changing conceptions of the nature of children and childhood (James and Prout 2003).

Thus, Scotland had led the way in relation to the issue of delinquency, making an important distinction between needs and deeds. However, implementation of its recommendations had to wait until the introduction of the Social Work (S) Act 1968 (under Part III) which followed the White Paper *Social work and the community* (Cmnd 3065: 1966) which addressed the issues concerning the organisation and delivery of social work services referred to in Chapter 1. In relation to children, young people and their families, local authorities (under the terms of s.12(2)) now had a specific (positive) duty to offer assistance to children, young people and their families where this appeared to diminish the need to either receive the child into their care or to refer the child to the children's hearing. Prevention was now seen as a primary function of the social work task.

Principles of the children's hearing system

The CHS is founded upon a number of key principles which were initially articulated by the Kilbrandon Committee and are still relevant today, with some amendments to reflect the experiences of the three decades of its operation:

- that the child who has offended and who may well be culpable is in as much need of care and protection as the child who may have been offended against;

- that the courts are not an appropriate forum in which to discuss what is best for a child and that a more informal setting and context should be provided;

- that what is best for the child can more usefully be determined by a careful and structured discussion of the situation which involves the child themselves, their parents/carers and other significant people in their lives (family, teachers, etc.);

- that the child is not considered in isolation from their broader circumstances; an holistic approach is essential (Bronfenbrenner 1979; Jack 2000) which does not limit the panel in the breadth or depth of its discussion;

- that what is important are the child's needs, not their deeds;

- that the hearing, whilst being more informal, still recognises the need for procedural fairness, accuracy and transparency;

- that the right of appeal exists to the Sheriff against any decision made by the hearing;

- that all proceedings are conducted in private (s.43);

- that the panel membership be constituted of lay volunteers (s.39).

In relation to the making of any decision concerning a child, there are three key principles which the hearings (and courts) have to consider (see ss.11(7) and 16, 1995 Act):

- that the welfare of the child is paramount (the 'welfare principle');

- that no order should be made in respect of a child unless it is absolutely essential (the 'no order principle');

- that every child should be given the opportunity to express their views and that children over the age of 12 are presumed to be sufficiently mature to be able to form a view (see Age of Legal Capacity (S) Act 1991 s.2 (4)).

It is worthwhile noting here that Articles 12(1) and 12(2) of the UN Convention on the Rights of the Child (UNCRC), which refer to the child's right to express their views and of state parties to ensure that opportunities are made available in judicial proceedings for this to happen, were operational in Scotland for more than 20 years prior to the UK government ratifying the convention itself, giving clear evidence of the forward-thinking nature of the Scottish system. However, the provisions of section 11(7) of the 1995 Act were enacted in order to formally bring Scots law into line with the requirements of Article 12 of the UNCRC.

The CHS was given effect by Part III of the Social Work (S) Act 1968 when it was implemented in 1971.

The structure and functions of the children's hearing system

Most of the legal provisions governing the CHS are contained within the 1995 Act, subsidiary legislation, rules, regulations, guidance and decisions of the Court of Session, all of which will be referred to as appropriate. The provisions of the Social Work (S) Act 1968 as they related to the CHS were repealed by the 1995 Act. It is also important to remember that there are a number of international or supra-state documents which relate to the CHS, notably the UNCRC, the ECHR (1950) as ratified by the implementation of the Human Rights Act 1998 (UK) and the 'Beijing Rules' (United Nations, 1985).

RESEARCH SUMMARY

International influences on the CHS

The UNCRC (United Nations 1989) was ratified by the UK government on 16 December 1991 and at the time had the effect of rendering some provisions of existing Scots law incompatible with the UK's new international obligations (see Chapter 1). The law in Scotland relating to children therefore required to be amended to take the effects of the UNCRC into account as well as recognising the changes which had taken place in society since the implementation of the Social Work (S) Act 1968. The Convention makes it explicit that all children have additional rights over and above those human rights enshrined within the ECHR and the Human Rights Act 1998 simply because of their special status as a child. The following are the main Convention articles which relate to the CHS:

Article 1: Definition of a child;
Article 2: Non-discrimination;
Article 3: The welfare of the child;
Article 5: Respect for the role of the family and recognition of the child's evolving capacities;
Article 9: The child's right to live with their parents;
Article 12: The child's right to participate in decision-making;
Article 18: Parental responsibilities;
Article 19: Protection from abuse and neglect;
Article 37: Protection from torture and issues of deprivation of liberty;
Article 40: Administration of juvenile justice (see 'Beijing Rules').

The ECHR (United Nations 1950) was ratified by the UK government in 1951 and has since been incorporated into all UK law via the implementation of the Human Rights Act 1998. Because the ECHR was not drawn up with the rights of children as one of its explicit objectives, not all of its articles are relevant to the CHS, although the following are:

Article 3: Prohibition of torture;
Article 5: Right to liberty and security;
Article 6: The right to a fair trial;
Article 8: The right to respect for private and family life;
Article 14: Prohibition of discrimination.

Continued

The United Nations Standard Minimum Rules for the Administration of Juvenile Justice (United Nations 1985) (the 'Beijing Rules') set out a broad range of fundamental principles by which member states of the UN should aim to promote and develop systems of juvenile justice which further the interests of such individuals. Article 40 of the UNCRC enhances the provisions of the Beijing Rules.

The personnel of the hearing

There are certain people who have a legal right and a duty to be present at a hearing and there are those whose attendance is determined by the chairperson. The 1995 Act makes it quite clear who these people are.

ACTIVITY 2.2

Here is a list of those people who are referred to in the 1995 Act in relation to attendance at a hearing. Indicate those you think have a duty to attend and those you think have a right to attend. Remember: if you have a duty to attend, you must; if you have a right to attend, you may do so, subject to certain conditions in some instances.

Panel members	*Unmarried father of the child*
The child's parents	*The Reporter*
Social worker	*Member of Scottish*
The press	*Committee on Tribunals*
The child	*Police/prison officer*
A safeguarder	*The child's teacher*
A representative of the child	*The child's best friend*
A legal representative of the child	*The child's GP*

Comment

There are a number of rules and regulations relating to who can, cannot, should and should not attend a children's hearing.

The Reporter

The Reporter has a duty to attend the hearing.

The panel members

The panel must be comprised of three people, with both a male and a female being present (s.39(5)). One of the panel members will chair the hearing and these individuals have a duty and a right to attend.

The child

The child has a duty and a right to attend the hearing (s.45), although the hearing may release the child from this obligation if they feel that their attendance would be detrimental to their interests, and this would be discussed at a business meeting (s.64) held prior to the hearing itself if a request to dispense with the child's attendance has been made.

Relevant persons
A 'relevant person' is defined in s.93(2)(b) of the 1995 Act and includes any parent enjoying parental responsibilities or parental rights as defined by Part I of the 1995 Act. It also relates to any person in whom parental responsibilities or rights are vested by the 1995 Act and any person who ordinarily (other than by reason of employment, so this would exclude childminders, for example) has charge of or control over the child (s.5 of the 1995 Act is relevant here). A relevant person has a duty and a right to attend, although there are circumstances where this obligation can be lifted.

A safeguarder
Under the terms of s.41 of the 1995 Act this is defined as any person appointed by the hearing to safeguard the interests of a child where there may be a conflict of interest. Any safeguarder has a right to attend all stages of a hearing.

A legal representative appointed for the child
Any legal representative appointed to represent the child at any stage of a hearing has a statutory right to attend. The whole issue of the legal representation of children in what is essentially a civil process is one which has arisen as a result of challenges to the CHS in respect of Article 6 of the ECHR which refers to the right to a fair trial. These changes were introduced by the Children's Hearings (Legal Representation) (S) Rules 2001.

Members of the Scottish Committee of the Council on Tribunals
These representatives of the Council attend as a means of offering a level of quality assurance in respect of the hearing and its processes. Section 43(3)(a) governs this and they have a right to attend.

A representative of the child and relevant person
Both the child and the relevant person(s) have the right to have someone accompany them to the CH. There are, however, rules which determine the particular arrangements here (r 11: The Rules).

The press
Any *bona fide* member of the press has a right to attend a hearing as an observer (s.43(3)(b)) although they are not allowed to publish any information which could lead to the child being identified and the hearing may exclude the journalist. These provisions are intended to strike a balance between the protection of privacy and the need to ensure that the hearing and its processes are as transparent as possible, in keeping with the requirements of Article 6 of the ECHR.

The police or a prison officer
Either of these may attend if they have in custody any person who is required to attend the hearing and security requires this.

The unmarried father of the child

Under the current arrangements, an unmarried father is not regarded as a relevant person for the purposes of attending the hearing and would therefore have neither a duty nor the right to attend. If, however, he is living with the child's mother he may attend although he is still not regarded as a relevant person. The whole issue of family law in Scotland, including the rights of the unmarried father, are currently being examined (Scottish Executive 2004a) and section 17 of the Family Law (Scotland) Bill, introduced to the Scottish Parliament in February 2005, would amend section 3 of the Children (S) Act 1995 concerning the parental responsibilities and rights of unmarried fathers. This may well have implications for issues relating to the CHS.

The social worker

The social worker does not have the right to attend, although their attendance may well be seen as necessary for the hearing to be able to proceed and they would therefore be instructed to attend. Given their involvement with the child and their family, it is often the case that the social worker has more to offer than most people present, particularly as a result of their involvement in the assessment process and the preparation of reports. The hearing can, however, proceed in the absence of the social worker if they feel that to do so would not prejudice the child's position.

Others

Potentially there is a range of other people who might usefully have something to offer to these proceedings. These might include other social workers, family support workers, health professionals, school staff, other relatives and friends and family of the child. We have to remember, however, that the relative informality of the hearing itself is designed to make it as easy as possible for the child to speak up and to take an active role in those proceedings which affect them; it has to be 'child-friendly'. Therefore, contributions may be made in other ways, usually through a report presented to the hearing, although there are certain rules governing this. However, if someone's presence is felt to be necessary for the proper consideration of the case, then they would be invited to attend.
(Scottish Executive 2003b)

The legal framework of the CHS

As mentioned above, the main piece of legislation governing the operation of the CHS is the Children (S) Act 1995. Part II of the 1995 Act, particularly Chapters 2 and 3, relate to the CHS. As well as this, there are a number of other statutes, regulations, guidance and rules which are applicable and have relevance. The main ones are noted below.

Statute

- Adoption (S) Act 1978

- Age of Legal Capacity (S) Act 1991

- Criminal Justice (S) Act 1995

- Human Rights Act 1998

- Anti-Social Behaviour etc. (S) Act 2004

Statutory Instruments, Rules and Regulations

- Children's Hearings (S) Rules 1996

- Children's Hearings (Transmission of Information etc.) (S) Regulations 1996

- Emergency Child Protection Measures (S) Regulations 1996

- Secure Accommodation (S) Regulations 1996

- Act of Sederunt (Child Care and Maintenance Rules) 1997

- Social Work (Panel of Persons to Safeguard the Interests of Children) (S) Regulations 2001

- Children's Hearings (Legal Representation) (S) Rules 2001

These have a pivotal role in relation to the CHS along with those international documents referred to above.

Case law/legal precedent

In Chapter 1, we spoke about the way in which the courts can interpret the application of the law in respect to particular cases as they are dealt with. When a matter is before the children's hearing there is a right of appeal. Any appeal would in the first instance be heard by the Sheriff in the Sheriff Court. If the finding of the Sheriff is appealed (and there are only certain circumstances in which this can be done), the matter will go before the Sheriff Principal or be heard in the Court of Session (see Chapter 1). Here, the judge(s) will make a ruling in respect of that original view. This is referred to as *case law* as it sets a precedent which overrides all other judgements on the matter and is legally binding on all lower courts unless and until a higher court reviews that decision. Thus, due process allows the matter to travel up the court system to the point where a decision may be made which affects the interpretation of the law as it relates to that issue. There are a number of significant pieces of case law which relate to the operation of the CHS and some of these are presented in the box below.

RESEARCH SUMMARY

Case law

Gillick v. West Norfolk and Wisbech Area Health Authority *[1985] 3 All E.R. 402 (HL): this English case set a major precedent for all UK law. In essence it heralded a shift away from parental rights towards children's rights. A mother objected to the family GP's decision to prescribe contraceptive medication to her daughter without informing her as the child's mother. The girl was under the age of 16. As a result of this decision (which has been tested many times) a child under the age of 16 in Scotland can agree or not to any form of medical treatment, providing they are deemed to be 'Gillick competent', which means that, in the opinion of a registered medical practitioner, they understand the nature and consequences of such treatment. These provisions have since been incorporated into section 2 (4) of the Age of Legal Capacity (S) Act 1991. The ruling also extends to issues of confidentiality and other matters.*

Continued

S v. Millar, 2001 S.L.T. 531: this ruling was the first ECHR challenge to the CHS and referred itself to McMichael v. United Kingdom (see below) and established that the child and the relevant person(s) must receive a 'fair hearing' within the terms of Article 6 of the ECHR. This means that the child and the relevant person(s) must have appropriate access to both the hearing and the appeal process including the right to legal representation in certain circumstances (The Children's Hearings (Legal Representation) (S) Rules 2002). The ruling also established that the CHS is to be seen as an independent tribunal which deals with civil and not criminal matters, the former restricting itself to issues relating to the child's welfare, the latter being concerned with punishment. This ruling also has a relevance to the underlying philosophy of the whole CHS and the principles espoused by the Kilbrandon Committee.

McMichael v. United Kingdom (1995) 20 E.H.R.R. 205: this case related to issues of the role and rights of the unmarried father of a child referred to the hearing. It was argued that the father's exclusion from the hearing and its processes on the grounds that he was not married to the child's mother was in fact discriminatory and contrary to Article 14 ECHR (prohibition of discrimination). Furthermore, and as a result of this exclusion, the father received no information about the case and was not party to the views expressed by the child at the hearing. It was argued that this was contrary to Articles 6 and 8 ECHR.

On appeal, it was held by the court that the parents of the child have the right to any information submitted to the hearing by the child. This has obvious implications for the management of the CHS and there are issues relating to the impact this disclosure may have upon the child, particularly if the disclosure of such information is damaging to the parent. In circumstances where there may be a risk to the child arising as a result of this disclosure, the hearing members would need to consider very carefully whether they have to take steps to afford the child appropriate protection. In reality, these situations are rare. One other implication of this ruling is that any papers relating to the hearing must be sent to the child (if over the age of 12 years) and to the relevant persons.

Standard of proof

In all proceedings relating to the CHS, the standard of proof to be followed is that relating to civil law and not criminal law. As mentioned in Chapter 1, civil law demands that the matter be proven on the balance of probability, which means that it was more likely to have happened than not. The standard of proof required in criminal matters is that of 'beyond all reasonable doubt'. Thus, a child who is referred to the CHS because they have committed an offence can have the matter established as 'fact' by the hearing operating on the basis that the offence was more likely to have been committed than not (on the basis of available evidence, although the offence ground only relates to those children over the age of criminal responsibility (8 years) as any child under this age is deemed to be incapable of committing an offence). It may seem that the child has been found 'guilty': they have not. It is only the courts which are concerned with issues of guilt/innocence and, recalling the principles of the CHS and the implications of *S* v. *Millar*, the issue is one which relates to the welfare of the child. Having offence grounds accepted by the hearing does not mean that the child has a criminal record. If, however, an offence ground is disputed at the hearing and the hearing decides not to discharge the referral, the matter would be referred to the Sheriff for proof (as with any disputed ground of referral). If this happens in relation to an offence ground, then the Sheriff has to consider the matter against the criminal standard of proof.

Making a referral to the Reporter

Who can refer a child to the Reporter?

The short answer is that anyone can. In reality however, it tends to be the local authority (social worker), the police, schools or other official personnel. However, the 1995 Act allows for any person at all, with what they believe to be just cause, to pass information to the Reporter, who will then decide whether to undertake further inquiries if they believe that one or more of the grounds of referral exist. Figure 2.1 explains the process.

The Referral Process

```
Stealing            CHILD IN TROUBLE            Neglected
Truanting                                       Abused
Glue-sniffing                                   Running away


School                                          Social Work Service
Police                                          Friend
Health Visitor      REFERRED BY ANYONE          Neighbour
Nursery school                                  Parents
Youth club                                      Child


                    TO THE REPORTER


Seeks report from social                        Looks at evidence to see
work and education                              if grounds can be proven
                    ARE THERE GROUNDS
                    FOR REFERRAL?
Reads police report                             May talk to parent/child
(as appropriate)    and
                    MAY THE CHILD BE IN
                    NEED OF COMPULSORY          Thinks about what is in
Studies other reports  MEASURES OF              the child's best interests
                    SUPERVISION
Uses information already                        Discusses the case with
available                                       others who might know
                                                about the family


HEARING NOT REQUIRED    NO      YES    REFERS CHILD TO A HEARING

                                       Reporter informs:

MAY REFER CHILD TO                     ● Child
LOCAL AUTHORITY FOR                    ● Relevant person(s)
VOLUNTARY ADVICE,                      ● Local authority or police if referred
GUIDANCE ASSISTANCE                      by one of them of his/her decision
                                         and course of action
```

Figure 2.1 *The process of referral to the reporter*

Source: Scottish Executive (2003b, p42)

Reproduced under the terms of Crown Copyright Policy Guidance issued by HMSO.

Grounds of referral

Section 52 of the 1995 Act refers to the grounds under which a child may be referred to the Reporter in order that consideration can be given as to whether the child is in need of compulsory measures of supervision. The whole of the section is reproduced below.

CHILDREN REQUIRING COMPULSORY MEASURES OF SUPERVISION

52. *(1) The question of whether compulsory measures of supervision are necessary in respect of a child arises if at least one of the conditions mentioned in subsection (2) below is satisfied with respect to him.*

(2) The conditions referred to in subsection (1) above are that the child:

(a) is beyond the control of any relevant person;

(b) is falling into bad association or is exposed to moral danger;

(c) is likely

> *(i)   to suffer unnecessarily; or*
> *(ii) be impaired seriously in his health or development, due to a lack of parental care;*

(d) is a child in respect of whom any of the offences mentioned in Schedule 1 to the Criminal Procedure (S) Act 1995 (offences against children to which special provisions apply) has been committed;

(e) is, or is likely to become, a member of the same household as a child in respect of whom any of the offences referred to in paragraph (d) above has been committed;

(f) is, or is likely to become, a member of the same household as a person who has committed any of the offences referred to in paragraph (d) above;

(g) is, or is likely to become, a member of the same household as a person in respect of whom an offence under sections 1 to 3 of the Criminal Law (Consolidation) (S) Act 1995 (incest and intercourse with a child by a step-parent or person in position of trust) has been committed by a member of that household;

(h) has failed to attend school regularly without reasonable excuse;

(i) has committed an offence;

(j) has misused alcohol or any drug, whether or not a controlled drug within the meaning of the Misuse of Drugs Act 1971;

(k) has misused a volatile substance by deliberately inhaling its vapour, other than for medicinal purposes;

(l) is being provided with accommodation by a local authority under section 25, or is the subject of a parental responsibilities order obtained under section 86, of this Act and, in either case, his behaviour is such that special measures are necessary for his adequate supervision in his interest or the interest of others.

Continued ▶

> *(3) In this part of the Act, 'supervision' in relation to compulsory measures of supervision may include measures taken for the protection, guidance, treatment or control of the child.*
>
> *(Section 52 of the Children (S) Act 1995 (c.36) is reproduced under the terms of Crown Copyright Policy Guidance issued by HMSO).*

You might find the way in which the grounds of referral are worded rather cumbersome. I have deliberately reproduced the whole section as it appears in the 1995 Act to give you a sense of what to expect. Don't be scared of 'legalese'; the more you are exposed to it, the less frightening it becomes.

ACTIVITY 2.3

Here I present a number of short vignettes for you to consider. With each of them, try to identify which of the grounds of referral mentioned in section 52 (2) of the 1995 Act could apply (and it might be more than one):

- *Sarah is 9. She attends school sporadically and when she does she is noted to be rather dirty, smelly and unkempt. She eats voraciously at lunch times and has been seen taking food and sweets from other children.*

- *Jacob is 3. His mum has recently met Peter who has a previous conviction for assault occasioned upon his own 5-year-old son.*

- *Adam is 7. He was recently assaulted by his father, suffering a broken arm as a result.*

- *Mary is 4. She is Adam's sister.*

- *Alice is 13. She is known to hang out with a gang of much older girls who frequent pubs in the local area which are known to turn a blind eye to their activities and seem to be used as venues for 'fencing' stolen goods. Her parents are aware of this but claim that Alice is 'fine'.*

- *John is 14. He regularly stays out overnight with 'friends' of whom his parents know nothing. They have said that he will do nothing they ask of him and he has hit his mum on several occasions and threatened to have his dad beaten up by his pals.*

- *Paul is 14. He smokes cannabis on a regular basis, which his parents feel is making him 'funny'. He also stole two bottles of vodka from the local supermarket. He has been offending on a regular basis.*

- *Phillip is 11. He can be seen most mornings wandering around the town centre with a group of older boys and two men, smoking cigarettes. His parents say they have tried everything to 'sort him out' but have now given up and couldn't care less.*

- *Mark is 12. He recently returned home from a friend's house appearing to be drunk, although no alcohol could be found. He did have an empty aerosol can in his school bag which he says was given to him by a man he visits.*

Continued

> • *Sasha is 13. She has been in foster care for several weeks following a disagreement with her parents. Everyone agreed that some time apart would help ease a difficult situation. Things are not going well in the placement and Sasha has run away several times, often meeting up with her friend Alice.*

Comment

The above scenarios are ones which you may come across in your practice and it is important for you to be aware of how situations you may well encounter can constitute grounds for referral to a hearing which would indicate that the child may be in need of compulsory measures of supervision:

• Sarah = s.52 (2) (c)

• Jacob = s.52 (2) (f)

• Adam = s.52 (2) (d)

• Mary = s.52 (2) (e)

• Alice = s.52 (2) (a), (b) and (c)

• John = s.52 (2) (a) and possibly (b)

• Paul = s.52 (2) (j), (i) and (a)

• Mark = s.52 (2) (k)

• Sasha = s.52 (2) (l) and possibly (b).

It is, however, important for you to remember that it is not the job of the social worker to draw up the grounds of referral: that is the role of the Reporter. The Reporter then has to specify the facts upon which the grounds are alleged to exist. Rather, it is for the social worker to be aware of how particular circumstances of which you might be aware could indicate that the child's situation requires a more formal approach to its management. This whole area concerning the issue of referral to the Reporter is being reviewed. It may be that new criteria are developed based upon tests of 'significant need' and 'the need for compulsion'. If referrals do not meet the criteria for compulsion then the Reporter may refer the matter back to the local authority for them to fulfil their duties towards the child (Scottish Executive 2005a).

What are compulsory measures of supervision?

In many instances, where you are not sure what a particular thing means in an Act you can turn to a section of it (usually near the end) entitled 'Interpretation'. This section will have a list of all the phrases and other terms used in the Act and a definition of them. For example, the various definitions of a child can be found in section 93 (2) of the 1995 Act. Similarly, the definition of a children's hearing can be found in section 93 (1), as can that of compulsory measures of supervision. However, some definitions are not really all that helpful and that relating to compulsory measures of supervision is one of them; it is rather tautologous (which means that it seems to go round in circles). However, if you look at section 70 of the Act you will find an explanation there.

Any supervision requirement is made in accordance with due process and with due consideration being given to the three overarching principles referred to above as well as having reference to the implications of Article 6 (1) (the right to a fair trial) and Article 8 (the right to private and family life) of the ECHR (as ratified by the Human Rights Act 1998 (UK)) and the imposition of the order must be consistent with the ECHR principle of *proportionality*. This rather grandiose term simply refers to the need for any action (in this case the imposition of a legal order on someone which may interfere with their rights under Article 8 of the ECHR) by a public authority (in this case the CHS) to be in proportion to its stated aim (in this case, the protection, guidance, treatment or control of the child (see s.52 (3)). This means that the hearing should not impose an order if it appears that not to do so could achieve the same ends just as effectively (which equates with the 'no order principle' referred to above).

What can the hearing do?

Once the decision has been taken to convene a hearing, all the arrangements will be put in place by the Reporter. The actual proceedings are governed by a number of rules and regulations, in particular the Children's Hearings (S) Rules 1996 (The Rules) and others, some of which have been referred to above.

The hearing really only has two options open to it once the grounds of referral have either been accepted (in part or in full) or established by the Sheriff: either to discharge the case (s.69 (12)) or to impose compulsory measures of supervision on the child (s.70). It can continue the case to a subsequent hearing if it feels that more information is required but in essence this option only leads back to the two options referred to initially.

Discharge of the referral

After they have considered the case before them (s.69 (1)), the hearing may decide that compulsory measures of supervision are not necessary and therefore discharge the referral. In reaching any decision the hearing will have taken into account the three overarching principles contained in section 16.

Compulsory measures: supervision requirements

If the hearing feels that it would be in the child's best interests to impose a supervision requirement, they have to consider what form that should take. Any supervision requirement lasts for one year. During that time the order can be reviewed at the request of the child or any other relevant person after three months (s.73 (6)) and in any case the matter will go before a hearing to review the situation within a year from the date the order was first made (s.73 (2)) and will automatically expire upon the child attaining 18 years of age (s.73 (3)) if this is sooner. If the situation concerning the child alters during the life of the order, the local authority may request a review hearing to consider discharging the order or, if things are not working well, to look at other options (s.73 (4)). Once the order has been made by the hearing, the local authority has a legal duty to implement or 'give effect' to the requirement (s.71). This duty has recently been given added force by the implementation of section 136 of the Anti-Social Behaviour etc. (S) Act 2004, which inserts a number of new requirements into sections 70 and 71 of the 1995 Act. This arose because of concerns surrounding the way in which local authorities interpreted their obligations under the 1995 Act regarding the implementation of supervision requirements and the way in which many orders were not implemented quickly enough, thus depriving the child of a necessary service.

There are basically two elements to a supervision requirement:

- where the child is to live (and therefore with whom) (s.70 (3) (a));

- that the child will comply with any condition(s) specified (s.70 (3) (b)).

The first element is the most significant, certainly from the perspective of the child. The implication is that the hearing may order that the child live either at home or elsewhere; this could be with relatives, friends, foster carers, in a residential establishment (a 'children's home') or in secure accommodation. All of these options are available to the hearing dependent upon the circumstances. In all cases, the requirement in terms of residence has to be proportional (see above). All of those options which might relate to the child living somewhere else other than at home are underpinned by a range of rules and regulations and if a child is looked after away from home, then there are a number of obligations placed upon the local authority and the provisions of section 17 of the 1995 Act would apply. We will be discussing these matters in more detail in Chapter 5 concerning children who live away from home.

In most cases, children who are made the subject of supervision requirements remain at home with their families. This is entirely in keeping not only with issues of proportionality, but also in keeping with the ethos of the 1995 Act, s.22 (1) (a) of which imposes a duty upon the local authority to promote the welfare of children in need in their area. This duty extends to the promotion of the child's upbringing within the context of their family (s.22 (1) (b)), as long as this is consistent with their other duty to promote their welfare. This is a good example of how societal views on what constitutes good practice in relation to particular groups of people are codified in legislation.

The supervision requirement will mean that the social worker and the child will work together to address those issues which were the reason for the hearing in the first place. Of necessity this will involve some work with the child's family, depending upon the age of the child and the issues to be addressed.

RESEARCH SUMMARY

Number of supervision requirements on 31 March 2004: (figures in paranthesis refer to the number as a percentage of total of children 'looked after' (11,700) which includes a range of other measures not referred to here).

> *Supervision requirement at home = 4,832 (41%)*
> *Supervision requirement away from home (foster care etc.) = 3,568 (31%)*
> *Supervision requirement in residential establishment = 808 (7%)*
> *Supervision requirement in secure accommodation = 51 (>1%)*

In order to place these figures in perspective, there were 11,700 children looked after by local authorities at 31 March 2004. This represents 1% of all children in Scotland under the age of 18 years.

> *Source: www.scotland.gov.uk/topics/statistics/16135/4401*

The supervision requirement may have a condition attached to it with which the child has to comply. This could mean that they have to attend a weekly group which will help them to look at their behaviour, or they might have to attend appointments with another professional to get help with managing anxiety, or they might have to be seen by a doctor. In the latter situation, there is a caveat; section 90 of the 1995 Act upholds the provisions of section 2(4) of the Age of Legal Capacity (S) Act 1991, which states that any child under the age of 16 (being the age of majority in Scotland) can consent to any surgical, medical or dental treatment or procedure providing they are capable of understanding the nature and proposed consequences of that procedure. It is important to remember that having the capacity to consent automatically brings with it the capacity to refuse consent. Any attempt to impose any form of treatment on a child who has refused to consent would constitute an assault.

The supervision requirement might also mean that the child cannot have any form of contact with some individual and the details of this would need to be specified in the order. Any condition which might be inserted into a supervision requirement must be one which can be implemented. For example, a condition on contact between a child and a parent which said that this should take place every Thursday between 11 o'clock and 2 o'clock would be too prescriptive, as well as being incompatible with a child attending school.

In all situations, any decision taken by the CHS must be guided by the three overarching principles referred to above, be in proportion to the aim of the exercise, be absolutely necessary, be workable and last only as long as is absolutely necessary.

CASE STUDY

Steven is 14 years old. You have been working with him for about six months now after he was referred to your department by his parents who were becoming increasingly concerned about his behaviour, his choice of friends and his poor school attendance. Things are not going too well for him at the moment. He has been excluded from school on a temporary basis because of fighting and his parents are worried about how things will end up. You agree with all parties that an intensive programme will be undertaken with Steven to address these issues; his parents are fully supportive of these plans and Steven is keen to sort things out, realising that he is on the 'slippery slope'.

ACTIVITY 2.4

Should Steven be referred to the Reporter? If so, what are the grounds of referral?

Do you think the Reporter will convene a hearing?

If yes, do you think the hearing would impose some kind of compulsory supervision?

If the hearing does not impose a supervision order, what factors might persuade them that this would be the correct course of action?

If the hearing does decide to impose a supervision order, what form might it take?

Comment

You have to make a judgement as to whether you think any of the grounds under section 52(2) exist once you have made the necessary inquiries, which you are obliged to do under section 53(1). Whatever you discover following your inquiry, you must pass to the Reporter. This may indicate to the Reporter that, in your judgement, inquiries were either unnecessary or that further measures may be required. It might be the case here that the grounds under section 52 (20) (a), (b) and (h) are relevant.

The Reporter has the option of calling a hearing if it is felt that any of the grounds under section 52 (2) exist. The first decision they have to make is whether to ask for more information (section 56 (1)) and this may lead to a request for a report from the local authority (section 53 (2)). On the basis of that report and any other information provided to or obtained by the Reporter, a decision will be made whether to convene a hearing or not. However, the mere presence of the existence of one or more of the grounds of referral does not mean that a hearing has to be convened. The Reporter has to be satisfied that, in conjunction with the presence of the grounds of referral, compulsory measures of supervision are necessary. In the end, it is the hearing members who will decide whether or not to impose some measure of supervision, not the Reporter.

If the Reporter decides to call a hearing in respect of Steven, both he and his parents will be advised of this (Rules 6 and 7 of the CH (S) Rules 1996).

On the basis of the information available to us at the moment, it might be the case that the hearing decides not to impose compulsory measures upon Steven. This may well be because of the arrangements that are being made by everyone and the fact that Steven himself seems to have recognised the need for things to change for the better. This would be a situation where the no order principle referred to above would carry a lot of weight. And don't forget that minimum intervention (often used synonymously with the notion of 'no order' equating with the minimum of intervention) does not necessarily mean that there should be minimum involvement in the child's life if the situation demands otherwise. Minimum intervention is entirely compatible with maximum involvement.

In relation to Steven's situation, it is also worth thinking about whether things would work out differently if, for example, he had not expressed a view that he felt things needed to change or if his parents had told you that they had 'had enough' and wanted no more to do with him, or that everyone had objected to the implementation of an intensive programme of work for Steven.

Serious and persistent offending

There are some children who present themselves as being more troubled and troublesome than others. Serious and persistent offending by children can be a symptom of many things, including child abuse, or it may be the result of a range of factors and influences including peer group pressure, family discord, poor parenting, the effects of poverty and social disadvantage (Rutter et al. 1998) or in some cases a simple, but somewhat misplaced, desire for excitement. In these situations the child may well find themselves before the hearing on a number of occasions because the measures in place (a supervision order, for example) appear to be having little effect upon their behaviour and the CHS may feel it can do little to improve the situation (Scottish Executive 1998a).

In these circumstances it is important to remember that the supervision order itself is purely a mechanism and a vehicle through which interventions can take place; the work undertaken by the social worker is what will have the effect, not the order. One of the issues that has been recognised (Audit Scotland 2002) is that there is a relative lack of specialist and suitably intensive programmes available for young serious and persistent offenders, recognising that persistent youth offending should be reduced because it 'creates a very real blight on the lives of too many individuals and communities in Scotland (and) represents a tragic waste and a lost opportunity to harness the skills and talents of many young Scottish people' (Jamieson 2002, p2). There clearly exists a political agenda in relation to this issue and we must remember that social work is a political activity, so don't be scared by this. What is important for you as a social worker is that it is your skills in working with children and young people that can make the rhetoric a reality.

In an attempt to strengthen the role of the CHS and in order to direct resources to the issue of serious and persistent offending, a number of initiatives have been established. Underpinned by a set of national standards for youth justice services (Scottish Executive 2002b), these included a pilot project of 'fast-track' hearings (Scottish Executive 2005b), which aimed to 'improve practice and outcomes with respect to the ways that the hearings system and associated services dealt with young people who persistently offend' (p1). In particular, the scheme sought to reduce the time taken to make decisions concerning each child and improve the quality of assessments, which were to include better risk assessments. It was further aimed to ensure that all young people who required access to a specialist programme to help in reducing their offending would get this. The evaluation of the project concluded that:

> *In short, the verdict from the evaluation on the effectiveness of fast track is definitely positive with regard to timescales and other aspects such as assessment and action plans, but not proven with regard to impact on offending* (ibid p30).

This suggests that there may well be issues concerning the quality of the programmes on offer to address these issues which may be affected by a number of factors including a lack of staff to do the work. It may also reflect a reality concerning the need for much earlier intervention into the lives of children and young people at the point before they begin to offend. This of course is never easy; predictive indicators of future offending behaviour do exist (Zigler et al. 1992; Rutter et al. 1998) but the decision to target resources at these issues should be seen in the context of the broader drive towards earlier and more effective interventions into the lives of children, young people and their families where there are early indications that things are not well (Scottish Executive 2005a).

Other measures looked at the establishment of a Youth Court scheme which has the flexibility to deal with 15- to 17-year-olds (Scottish Executive 2005c) as well as a review of the scope for using Restriction of Liberty Orders, Anti-Social Behaviour Orders (ASBOs) and Community Reparation Orders as well as the use of Parenting Orders (Scottish Executive 2004b), all of which are legislated for in the Anti-Social Behaviour etc. (S) Act 2004.

How effective these measures are likely to be is as yet not established. Their efficacy is as much to do with the principles (United Nations 1985, 1989) and resources underpinning them as it is to do with the skills and attributes of individual workers and teams and the nature of the child or young person's difficulties and their particular situation. What they do offer are further options which can be utilised; whether they turn out to be effective overall is yet to be seen, but the key lies in how effective it is for each individual, and no one initiative or strategy is likely to guarantee total success. What is more likely to be of benefit in the long run is effective social work practice which utilises all those options which have something to offer the child or young person. If it works for that child, then use it; if it doesn't, use something else. But in the midst of all of this we have to remember that underpinning all of this is relationships between people. And you, the social worker, are where it can all begin.

C H A P T E R   S U M M A R Y

This chapter has introduced you to the children's hearing system, its history and evolution, personnel, structures and basis in law. We have looked at the reasons for a child being referred to the hearing and some of the things the hearing can do. We have also considered some of the limitations of the CHS and looked at what is being done at the moment to deal with some difficult issues being faced by the system. We have also looked at the importance of international law and other guidance on the CHS as well as thinking about the importance of the three overarching principles which guide the hearing's decision-making.

FURTHER READING

McNorrie, **K** **McK** (2005) *Children's hearings in Scotland (2nd edition)*. Edinburgh: W. Green and Sons.

This is a rather technical book but will tell you all you ever wanted to know about the operation of the CHS.

Scottish Executive (2003) *The Children's Hearing System in Scotland: Training Resource Manual (2nd edition)*. Edinburgh: Scottish Executive.

This is a good place to start a more detailed exploration of the CHS.

WEBSITES

www.scra.gov.uk

www.childrens-hearings.co.uk

Good sites to visit and spend time on.

Chapter 3

Working with and providing support to children, young people and their families

A C H I E V I N G   A   S O C I A L   W O R K   D E G R E E

This chapter will help you to meet the following Scottish Standards in Social Work Education (SiSWE) (Scottish Executive 2003a: available at www.scotland.gov.uk/library5/social/ffsw.pdf).

Key Role 1: Prepare for, and work with, individuals, families, carers, groups and communities to assess their needs and circumstances.

1:1 Preparing for social work contact and involvement.

1:2 Working with individuals, families, carers, groups and communities so they can make informed decisions.

1:3 Assessing needs and options in order to recommend a course of action.

Key Role 2: Plan, carry out, review and evaluate social work practice with individuals, families, carers, groups, communities and other professionals.

2:1 Identifying and responding to crisis situations.

2:2 Working with individuals, families, carers, groups and communities to achieve change, promote dignity, realise potential and improve life opportunities.

2:3 Producing, implementing and evaluating plans with individuals, families, carers, groups, communities and colleagues.

2:4 Developing networks to meet assessed needs and planned outcomes.

Key Role 3: Assess and manage risk to individuals, families, carers, groups, communities, self and colleagues.

3:1 Assessing and managing risks to individuals, families, carers, groups and communities.

3:2 Assessing and managing risk to self and colleagues.

Key Role 4: Demonstrate professional competence in social work practice.

4:1 Evaluating and using up-to-date knowledge of, and research into, social work practice.

4:2 Working within agreed standards of social work practice.

4:4 Promoting best social work practice, adapting positively to change.

Key Role 5: Manage and be accountable, with supervision and support, for their own social work practice within their organisation.

5:3 Contributing to the management of resources and services.

5:4 Managing, presenting and sharing records and reports.

Introduction

This chapter considers the issue of working with and providing support to children, young people and their families. We shall look at what we mean by support, what types of support are available, the reasons why support might be required and how you might deliver that support.

Working with and supporting children, young people and their families is about practice. The previous chapters looked at the broader context within which your practice takes place: the legal and policy context and the framework provided by the children's hearing system. This chapter concentrates on doing social work. But we look at doing social work in a way which highlights a number of important themes and issues which relate to your practice, including relevant theoretical perspectives and policy and practice initiatives currently informing child care social work in Scotland.

The context for your practice

As a social worker working with children, young people and their families it is very important that you are clear about the nature of the work. Childcare social workers have very specific statutory responsibilities of which they must be aware and be able to perform. These include responding to allegations of child abuse and neglect (Chapter 4) and providing a service to those children and young people who are either looked after or accommodated by the local authority (Chapter 5). What this means is that whatever else you might do in your work, these duties supersede all other activity. Your prime responsibility is to the child or young person and the promotion of their welfare.

This has implications for your practice. If you are a social worker employed by the local authority, then these statutory responsibilities may well constitute the bulk of your caseload. Being involved in the investigation of child abuse and neglect and visiting and working with looked after and accommodated children can sometimes make it seem like there is little time left to do anything else. Spending time with a child talking through their worries and concerns or helping a single mum to cope with the demands of four pre-school children may be something you feel you don't have the time or the space to do. These issues represent many of the realities of childcare social work today and may well present you with challenges to your stamina, your values and your sense of what social work is all about.

As we saw in Chapter 1, social work and its activities has moved between different orientations at different points in time. These shifts can be typified as existing on a continuum (see Figure 3.1) with a child welfare orientation at one end and a child protection orientation at the other (Spratt 2001).

One of the tensions common within childcare social work is that of *care* versus *control* (Thompson 2005). Social workers have to constantly balance the need to work in partnership with the family whilst recognising that the needs of the child are paramount and that at times these may be in conflict with those of their family. In situations where a child needs to be protected, the responsibilities of the social worker are clear: action needs to be taken to afford the child the necessary protection. This is a situation where control has to be asserted. In other situations, working with a child may well be able to proceed within the context of a partnership with the family, thus being seen as caring. However, you may find that you have to recommend that a young person be placed in a secure unit and deprived of their liberty because they are out of control and getting involved in criminal activity. Are you being caring or are you controlling? You might argue that by recommending this course of action you are caring, because if something is not done to stop the behaviour, the young person would get into more trouble and continue to put themselves and others at risk. Similarly, in working with a young child and their parents who are struggling to cope and meet basic needs, at what point do you have to have recourse to the law to impose some control on the situation to try to make sure things change? Your role in offering support and of being caring may suddenly have to shift into one of control, where you enforce the law or other forms of agency policy. These actions represent forms of social control and at times may seem to run counter to your view as to what social work is all about. These tensions are real and you need to be aware of them and be in a position to respond to them within the context of your daily practise.

Figure 3.1 *Childcare orientations*

As we shall see, there is a plethora of policy documentation and practice initiatives currently operational in Scotland which attempt to respond to the many tensions inherent within modern family life as well as attempting to adhere to the modernisation agenda whereby all public services are as responsive as possible to individual need as well as being integrated, accountable and transparent. The current policy agenda attempts to integrate all those services which have relevance to children, young people and their families. The report *For Scotland's children: better integrated children's services* (Scottish Executive 2001a) is the template against which service planning and delivery take place within Scotland at this time. The report emphasises the following as being central to the planning, design, development, organisation and delivery of services to children by all providers and agencies:

- to consider children's services as a single service system;

- to establish a joint children's service plan;

- to ensure inclusive access to universal services;

- to coordinate needs assessment;

- to coordinate intervention;

- to target services.

(Scottish Executive 2001a, p73)

These factors are seen as being crucial to the achievement of a policy and practice context which ensures that children are safe, nurtured, healthy, and able to achieve, be active, respected, responsible and included in all aspects of society appropriate to their age.

In Scotland, the current policy framework attempts to be representative of both those orientations referred to above. There are numerous policy statements and initiatives emphasising prevention and support as well as major policy directives and legislation relating to the protection of children from abuse and neglect. In many respects the focus should rest somewhere near the middle of our continuum.

The practitioner's response to this, however, may be somewhat different as the reality on the streets is one often typified by crisis intervention and responses to child protection referrals (see Chapter 4) with little time or space being visible to do any preventative work or to intervene early before things reach crisis point. Staff shortages and a lack of resources at the level of practice are not untypical and represent the tensions which exist between the rhetoric of policy and the realities of practice. To be blind to these realities is to present an unrealistic view of social work in the 21st century. It needs to be acknowledged that social work *per se* is a challenging occupation and childcare social work in particular is often seen as a high-risk occupation. This is because the stakes can be high and there have been numerous tragedies over the years where children have been severely abused and even killed at the hands of their parents and carers (Corby et al. 2001; Hammond 2001; Laming 2003; O'Brien et al. 2003; Reder et al. 1993), with social workers often being in the firing-line, damned if they do and damned if they don't. These events often drive the agenda for change and in Scotland this has been the case over the past few years. As we shall see in Chapter 4, these events have prompted major initiatives and change in the area of child protection.

These issues of course reflect the challenges of family life today, and are in their way influenced by the various discourses (or debates) within society concerning the status of children (Fionda 2001), the role of the family (Dingwall et al. 1983) and the very purpose of social work and welfare provision itself. In relation to policy and practice, the dominant discourses of law, economics and medicine can be seen to be influential, as can those which form the backdrop of much social work activity in the field of childcare, those from psychology and sociology, along with other emerging discourses from service user groups (Healy 2005). As we shall see, these influence both policy and practice in many ways and it is helpful to try to identify which of these (and there may be more than one having an influence at any one time) are informing policy and practice at any given time.

RESEARCH SUMMARY

Discourses in social work

Healy (2005) describes a number of discourses which influence social work in a number of ways. Some of these she describes as being more dominant than others.

Medicine: a powerful discourse often referred to as the 'medical model'. This sees all difficulties in terms of individual pathology. Key themes are diagnosis and treatment. Its influence is pervasive in social work, especially in those areas where there is a medical element to the service, for example, in mental health services and forensic medical investigations in situations of child abuse and neglect. Its strengths lie in the fact that

Continued ▷

47

medical interventions do save lives and treatments do work. One of its drawbacks in relation to social work is that it tends to ignore wider structural and situational factors which
may well be causal in terms of difficulties experienced by your clients. For example, being
depressed does have a biochemical component in terms of causation, but so does living in
very poor housing with little money and being the victim of racial abuse.

The law: *this too is a powerful discourse which has an influence on all aspects of social
work. In childcare social work its influence is obvious; practice is framed by legislation and
policy too is generated within those same parameters. The law is seen as being objective,
neutral, impersonal and impartial, its processes and outcomes based solely upon adher-
ence to the facts. The law also demands that social processes and people's lives conform
to distinct categorisations; for example, you are either guilty or not guilty, although in
Scotland there is a 'not proven' verdict. One important element of the power of the legal
discourse is that, within the practice context, the fulfilment of legal duties and responsibilities has precedence over other aspects of practice, as we have already referred to above.*

Economics: *economics as a discipline is concerned with the allocation of resources. Social
work services are subjected to the rigours of economic doctrines on an almost daily basis. All
service providers have to balance the books and get best value. At the individual level, the
social work task in certain areas of practice is very much focused on the commissioning and
purchasing of services which are then delivered (provided) by another worker or agency
who may or may not be a social worker. This purchaser/provider split has been evident for a
number of years consequent primarily upon the introduction of the NHS and Community
Care Act 1990 (UK). Latterly, the introduction of Direct Payments to clients via section 12b of
the Social Work (S) Act 1968 (as amended by s.7 of the Community Care and Health (S) Act
2002), which allows people to purchase the services they need from whichever service
provider they wish on the open market, heralds a further development in the provenance of
economics within social work and social care. Within childcare social work, the explicit pur-
chaser/provider split is perhaps not quite as evident, although clearly at the wider
organisational level social work services are purchased from other providers. For example,
residential school places, places in secure units and some counselling services are purchased
by authorities on either an individual or a block basis. At the wider macro-level, authorities
allocate government funding to different service areas and have to balance increasing levels
of need and demand with (often) diminishing financial allocations.*

Psychology: *this discourse is probably the one most familiar to you and to most practitioners. The various theories concerning psychological development are deeply embedded
within much of the social work literature and these inform many policy and practice initiatives. The theories of attachment (Bowlby 1997; Howe 2005), behaviourism (Smith et al.
2003), psychoanalysis (Freud 1991) and cognition (Piaget and Inhelder 1969, Flavell 1985)
all influence how we think about what we do and how we do it. For example, the oft-
used phrase 'age and stage of development' refers directly to Piaget's stage theory of
cognitive development and the notion of the child's level of maturity (see for example
ss.16(2) and 17(4) of the Children (S) Act 1995) also draws from psychological theorising
about the role of maturation in relation to cognition. All qualifying social work education*

Continued

courses include the study of human growth and development, the bulk of which draws from psychological theory. These ideas have been criticised for having an overly individualistic focus upon human growth and development, sometimes not recognising the broader social factors which have an effect on us; this has been particularly true in relation to psychoanalysis. However, the dominant practice approaches today tend to integrate aspects of psychology, sociology and other social sciences into the psychosocial approach.

Sociology: *this discourse is one which recognises the influence and impact of the social in social work. Sociology's focus upon the structure and functioning of society and its impact upon people contributes significantly to our understanding of the 'person in their environment'. For example, studies of poverty have highlighted the devastating effects this can have on people's lives (Rowntree 1901; Townsend 1979) as well as the impact of racism, class and other social phenomena. Sociology has also contributed to the ways in which we think about reality itself (Berger and Luckman 1979; Searle 1995) and how it is constructed in different ways for and by different people at different times. These themes within sociology have had an important bearing upon the development of labelling theory (Becker 1963) which has been used to challenge the perceived orthodoxy of medical and welfare professionals.*

Service user/alternative discourses: *the service user discourse emerged during the 1970s and has gathered strength over the intervening years. These views seek to challenge many of the dominant ideas which emerge from medicine and other discourses which seek to label and pathologise individuals as well as seeking a voice for the recipient of services in relation to their design and delivery. These discourses have become increasingly evident across all service user groupings, although they are more visible in relation to some groups than others (for example, people with learning disabilities and mental health service user groups), perhaps emphasising the powerful role of advocacy. In relation to children and young people, the children's rights discourse is becoming more and more prominent. Other discourses which are of increasing relevance are those which relate to the importance of religion, spirituality and alternative lifestyles.*

Who needs support and why?

Family life can be great fun. It can also be very difficult. Why is this? There are as many reasons as there are people, but some of us have the resources, both personal and material, to cope; many do not and as a result their capacity to function, develop and grow within generally accepted parameters is compromised.

Those people who may well seek out or otherwise require support in relation to childcare matters come from across the socioeconomic spectrum. It is recognised, however, that many will be those whose own resources are limited, personally, socially and economically (Ghate 2002; Statham and Holtermann 2004; Waterhouse et al. 2000) and they tend to be individuals and families functioning on the margins of society. Child poverty in particular is a major cause for concern in Scotland (Scott et al. 2005) as it is in other parts of the UK.

Reasons why people might need support

Poverty	*Mental health problems*	*Disability*
Housing problems	*Domestic violence*	*Child abuse*
Drug misuse	*Childcare problems*	*Racism*
School problems	*Relationship problems*	*Unemployment*
Parenting problems	*Alcohol misuse*	*Health problems*

These are just some of the reasons why support might be required. See if you can think of any more or unpick some of the categories mentioned above. For example, what might living in poverty actually mean on a day-to-day basis? The study by Waterhouse et al. (2000) mentioned above offers some interesting information concerning this very relationship. They found that of 1,155 children referred to the children's hearing, 55% came from families who were dependent upon state benefits as the major source of family income and 72% lived in local authority housing. These are but two of a number of key indicators of deprivation (www.scotland.gov.uk/library5/social/siod.pdf).

Comment

All of the above may occur in isolation and create situations which add pressure to the tasks of daily living. In some circumstances a number of these things occur together and become cumulative, triggering further difficulties. It is often the case that these circumstances are linked to poorer outcomes for children in terms of life-chances and general development (Rutter 1995). We would refer to these as *risk factors*. The provision of support to a child, young person and their family would aim to offset the effects of these and aim to promote *resilience* (Newman and Blackburn 2002).

Resilience

The notion of resilience is a theme very current in social work with children, young people and their families. In essence, resilience refers to the capacity to 'bounce back' and overcome adversity (Fonagy et al. 1994). Much research has been undertaken highlighting those factors which appear to be associated as risk factors for poorer life-chances and difficulties in later life. A number of these are noted in the box above and impact upon individuals, families and communities. The idea of promoting resilience, which may offset the negative effects of these factors and therefore be protective, has gained considerable currency. Research has identified a number of protective factors which seem to promote resilience (Gilligan 1999, 2000; Rutter 1985, 1995). For a set of useful and very practical guides to resilience see Daniel and Wassell (2002) and for an excellent review of the literature concerning this topic see Newman and Blackburn (2002).

Resilience factors: child

Stable and even temperament	*Good social skills*
A secure attachment	*Good communication skills*

Continued

A supportive family	*Flexible coping strategies*
A sense of autonomy	*Capacity to use humour*
A sense of positive self-worth	*Appropriately affectionate*

Resilience factors: family

Close, supportive relationships	*Consistency of care*
Close ties with alternative caregivers	*Consistency of routine*
Appropriate boundaries in place	*Lack of family discord*
Sufficient material resources	*Encouragement*
Emotional availability of caregivers	*Positive role models*

Resilience factors: community

A range of friends	*Safe living space*
Positive school experiences	*Wide support network*
Access to leisure facilities	*Good housing*
Involvement in organised activities	*Clear value base*
Good quality of life	*Safe public space*

Who provides services to children, young people and their families?

There are a range of agencies and professionals that provide services to children, young people and their families. In Scotland, as in other parts of the UK, legislation acts as the main framework within which services are conceived, configured and delivered. Of significance to us is section 22 of the Children (S) Act 1995 which states that local authorities shall (which means they must) 'safeguard and promote the welfare of children in their area who are in need' (s.22(1)(a)) and, 'so far as is consistent with that duty, promote the upbringing of such children by their families' (s.22(1)(b)), 'by providing a range and level of services appropriate to the children's needs' (s.22(1)). This means that local authorities are obliged to provide services in their area consistent with the level of need, although how and to what extent these are provided is left to each local authority to determine. Section 21 of the 1995 Act goes further in recognising that there are a range of other service providers who may well have services which could be of benefit to children, young people and their families. This would include health services. If the local authority feels that these other providers ('appropriate person(s)') could assist them 'in the exercise of any of their functions' (s.21(1)), then they simply have to ask. If the local authority asks, the provider is under an obligation to provide. This means that the local authority has to make arrangements with other providers to ensure that service delivery is tailored to local need and targeted appropriately and efficiently. Section 19 of the Children (S) Act 1995 obliges local authorities to produce and publish plans which specify those services which are available. Recent initiatives arising from the publication of *For Scotland's children* (Scottish Executive 2001a) now mean that all children's service plans have to be integrated with the service plans of other providers, creating a holistic framework for service delivery.

Social work departments: there are 32 local authorities across Scotland and all of these have a social work department. Nowadays, these may be combined with other local authority departments (education, housing) or in fact called something other than a social work department (Children's Services Department) but all of these employ social workers to visit and work with families as well as arranging and coordinating the delivery of services. They also provide a range of other services, such as family centres, where children, young people and their families can go in order that they might work together on learning new skills or attending a group looking at particular issues within the family which need to be addressed. The social work department also provides a substitute care service for those children who, for many reasons, are unable to live at home and a child protection service.

Education departments: these are part of the local authority and are responsible for providing education services to all children. These include primary and secondary education, pre-school services (toddler groups, nurseries) as well as a range of more specialist services such as psychologists, learning support for pupils with additional support needs and behavioural support units for pupils with challenging behaviours.

The Children's Hearing System: see Chapter 2.

NHS Health Boards: there are 15 Health Boards in Scotland providing a range of health related services. These include the more obvious hospital services as well as a range of specialist services such as school health services and Child and Adolescent Mental Health Services (CAMHS).

Housing departments: these exist as part of the local authorities as well as being formed in partnership with a number of housing associations. Their main remit relates to the provision of housing and related support. They play an increasingly important role in relation to those young people who have been looked after by the local authority (see Chapter 5) and are moving on to live on their own. This transition is an important one and the housing authorities can play a large part in supporting young people at this time.

Third sector organisations/voluntary organisations: there are many voluntary organisations in Scotland which provide a range of services. These range from one-to-one support for children, group-based work and a range of residential services, including schools. These organisations range in size from small locally based initiatives to large national charitable organisations (National Audit Office 2005).

Private sector: the private sector plays an increasingly important role in delivering services, particularly in relation to highly specialised residential services and some specialised counselling services.

What types of services and supports are available?

In the UK there are varying types of public services in place aimed at providing support to all of us. Some examples would be health care services (GPs, hospitals), education services (schools, nurseries), leisure services (libraries, museums, swimming pools), housing services (social housing), employment services (job centres), legal services (police, the courts), and social or welfare-based services (residential care homes, social workers), all of which exist as a framework to assist us in living out our daily lives. Access to these services is generally seen to be universal, meaning that if you need them, you can get them. In addition to these universal services are a range of tiered services which are more specialist, aimed at meeting more specific needs, and in this respect they are often referred to as being targeted. These might include specialist health care services (cardiology, mental health services), specialist education services (for children with specific learning needs) and social work services (fostering and adoption; child protection).

Access to these specialist services is obviously dependent upon your need for them. They are still universal in the sense that they are open to all, but access is restricted to those who really do need them. Thus, public service provision adopts (at least in theory) the principle of universality with regard to availability, but not necessarily in relation to accessibility.

It is, however, important to remember that public service provision, whilst ideally being needs-led is often resource-led. What this means is that people may have to wait for a service simply because there are not enough of them to go round. This might be because there are not enough staff to deliver the service or because there is no money to pay for it. If you refer a child to a specialist mental health service (CAMHS), there may be a waiting list. This has implications for you as a practitioner as well as for the family because your intervention may be influenced by service availability. This is very much a reality today; resources are finite and there are often competing demands upon local authorities and other welfare organisations to provide services to many different client groupings. Determining who should get what, when and for how long is a constant theme in social work and other services today and reflects the changing nature of society and of need. The whole issue of needs is one which permeates all aspects of service design and delivery and Maslow's hierarchy of needs (1970) is a good starting point for thinking about this (see Figure 3.2).

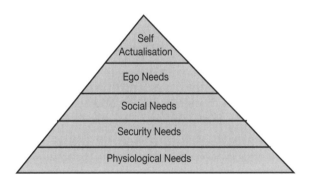

Figure 3.2 *Maslow's hierarchy of needs*

The types of need referred to here underpin our capacity to function and if these are not met at a particular level, higher-order needs are forgotten about until these are met. The need for food and water overrides all others, including the need for safety. If you are starving, then you will do some dangerous things to get food and water. Once you have these basic physiological needs met, then you look to have those at the next level met, and so on up to the top. If the needs of a lower level are not met, everything else is effectively put on hold until they are.

Some children find themselves unable to get their basic needs met and are therefore under threat. In the first instance they would turn to their parents or primary caregivers in order to have these needs met or to be protected, and most would receive it. However, some won't receive it either because their caregiver can't or won't protect them or because that very person may well be the source of danger itself. In these circumstances, the child would be in need of protection. It is useful to think of what the child needs as being laid out along a continuum, as shown in Figure 3.3.

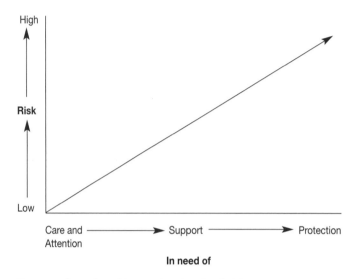

Figure 3.3 *A continuum of need and increasing levels of risk*

Being in need of care refers to that attention normally required by and given to any child at a given age. If a child is in need of support, this would imply that they have a range of additional needs which require additional attention. If a child is in need of protection, this implies that they are in danger and there is no one to protect them when they need this. This might include a child who is beaten by a carer or who is not fed very well. It might also mean that a child is being sexually abused or is behaving in a way which is dangerous for them; for example, they might be playing truant from school and getting involved in criminal activity.

In all of these situations a child has a need for something. Being in need of appropriate care and attention is part of being a child. Being in need of extra support if things are difficult is also part of the life of some children and this is why services are available. Sadly, being in need of protection is also a part of some children's lives and specialist services exist to deal with this, and these will be considered in the next chapter. As you can see from Figure 3.3, as the type of need changes, there is an increase in the level of risk to the well-being of the child or young person.

Look at the case scenarios below and identify who is in need of care, who is in need of support and who is in need of protection.

William is 3 weeks old. He lives with his mum, dad and older sister, Anne, who is 3. His mum does not work, preferring to stay home with the children.

John is 8 years old. He lives with his mum and her new boyfriend, Billy. John rarely goes to school and gets hit by Billy when he has been drinking. His mum does not bother about this.

Michael is 13. He lives with his dad and two younger brothers, Darren (10) and Lee (7). At times he is left to look after his brothers for a few hours whilst dad goes to the supermarket for the shopping.

Michelle is 14. She lives with her mum and dad. Her mum hits her a lot and her dad makes her sleep with him when mum is working away from home. She does not like this.

Kate is 15. She lives with her mum and younger brother Adam who is 7. She is studying for her exams at the moment but is upset because she has fallen out with her best friend.

Sarah is 6 years old. She lives with her mum and dad. She was recently excluded from school for swearing at the teacher and hitting another child with a shoe.

Comment

William is in need of that care appropriate to his age and stage of development.

John is in need of protection. His main caregiver appears not to be providing this for him.

Michael is in need of support (as are his brothers). It looks like dad is struggling to cope and needs time to himself but hasn't any appropriate support.

Michelle is in need of protection.

Kate is in need of care appropriate to her needs at that time.

Sarah is in need of support. She appears to be struggling to cope at school.

In those scenarios involving Michael and his brothers and Sarah, there is a need for support because the demands upon the family are greater than normal for a number of reasons. In relation to John and Michelle, protection is required as there are elements of the situation which are a cause for concern above and beyond that which might ordinarily be seen.

Within the context of current legislation, what being 'in need' means is defined in section 93 (4) of the Children (S) Act 1995 and refers to any child who 'is unlikely to achieve or maintain, or to have the opportunity of achieving or maintaining, a reasonable standard of health and development unless there are provided for him ... services by a local authority'. Furthermore, a child is also deemed to be in need under the 1995 Act if 'his health or development is likely significantly to be impaired, or further impaired, unless such services are so provided' or 'he is disabled' or is 'affected adversely by the disability of any other person in his family' or if the child is looked after by the local authority.

However, what being in need implies is an appreciation of what we mean by that very term itself, and this is sometimes contested. Bradshaw (1972) refers to four types of need as mentioned in the following research summary and these can be useful in thinking about this issue.

RESEARCH SUMMARY

In his seminal paper, 'The concept of social need', Bradshaw outlined four different ways of describing need.

Normative need: *this is what the expert or professional would define as need relative to a normal standard (e.g. enough food). Anything below this and you would be seen to be in need.*

Felt need: *this is need equated with want.*

Expressed need: *felt need (or a want) turned into action i.e. someone asks for or demands something.*

Comparative need: *need is determined by studying the characteristics of those in receipt of a service. If people with similar characteristics are not in receipt of a service, they are in need.*

Bradshaw details the interrelationships between the four definitions and this taxonomy is useful when service providers are studying or planning to meet social need.

Providing support as a social worker

In this section, I want to look at how you might work with children, young people and their families, and what form that work and support might take.

When considering the issue of support, we must also think about the nature of our practice (Horner 2003; Thompson 2005) and those theories which underpin it. Payne (2005, pp5–13) refers to three types of theory:

- theories about what social work is: these refer to things like the nature of welfare, why we have it and how we should deliver it;

- theories about how social work is done: these *practice theories* refer to things such as what is the best way to help somebody?;

- theories which offer knowledge to social work about the world (for example, psychology, sociology, etc.) which can be used to inform your understanding of certain things.

All of these theories interact with each other. What you do, based on what your agency agrees its role is in relation to children, young people and their families at any given time, is influenced by your understanding of people and their psychology as well as social institutions and how these act and interact.

Healy (2005), in describing this very thing, says that 'the deeply contextual and varied character of social work practices means that, in each practice encounter, we are involved in constructing and negotiating social work practice' (p4). She refers to a dynamic model of social work and sees this as being composed of four main elements:

- the institutional context of practice: the legislation, regulations, guidance and other organisational policies and procedures which essentially frame your practice;

- the formal professional base of social work: the values, knowledge and skills of the profession disseminated through social work education and other academic channels;

- your sense of practice purpose: the interplay between your formal purpose (what you are employed to do), your values and the impact of your interactions with clients on your view of what you are doing;

- the framework for practice: the interplay between formal knowledge and skills (including the institutional context) and the informal 'on-the job' knowledge and skills developed through your practice encounters (pp4–6).

Thinking about social work in this way enables you to understand how practice is made up and how each part interacts with, informs and influences the other.

It is crucially important for you to remember that when you are working with and offering support to children, young people and their families you must:

- offer and provide support within current legislative, policy and practice contexts;

- utilise yourself as a source of support by recourse to your interpersonal skills including effective, open and honest communication;

- reflect upon what you do, why, when, where and how;

- approach the task systematically and utilise the social work process to assess, plan, implement and evaluate your intervention(s);

- utilise available evidence on what works (evidence-based practice);

- involve children, young people and their families at every possible stage, remembering at all times that the needs of the child are paramount;

- record what you do (and what you don't do) openly, honestly and reflectively;

- draw upon all appropriate and available resources for your clients and for yourself in terms of advice, guidance, assistance and support;

- recognise your limitations and know when to seek help;

- remember that social work is what social work does.

These points are important and you should try to adopt these as central to your approach to practice.

Theory into practice

In this section, I want to look at using theory to inform practice in relation to the case study in Activity 3.2 below. The approaches I refer to here are offered as being broadly representative of the practice focus of much work with children, young people and their families in Scotland today.

Psychodynamic approaches

These approaches have the individual as their focus, particularly inner thoughts and feelings. Influenced by the psychodynamic theories of Freud and his followers, this approach concentrates on using observations of people's behaviour to interpret what is going on in their mind. In this respect, thoughts and feelings are seen to influence actions because of the presence of various internal drives, instincts and other mechanisms which are constantly at play. Difficulties in terms of day-to-day functioning are seen as being the result of negative early experiences which have not been resolved internally. Negative feelings are said to be repressed but they then seep out and manifest as undesirable behaviour, anxiety, depression and other forms of psychopathology. Interventions would seek to highlight the nature of the person's early experiences and encourage them to talk about these. By doing this, the person can hopefully gain a degree of insight into the effect these experiences have had on them and may be able to work towards resolving them. As a result, the negative manifestations of these inner conflicts would diminish and the person would be able to cope effectively again. Many counselling services use this approach, exclusively or in conjunction with other methods.

Psychosocial approaches

These approaches can be seen to be developments of and extensions from psychotherapeutic approaches. These place emphasis upon the influence of the social environment upon the individual and the here and now rather than the sole influence of early experience. Perhaps the most widely referred to formulation is that of Hollis (Woods and Hollis 1990) and psychosocial casework. In this formulation, inner thoughts and feelings are seen as being important but are not allowed to overshadow the impact of the current situation and the effect they have on thoughts and feelings. In many ways, this approach uses a range of ideas from psychoanalysis and other disciplines to create a more pragmatic approach to the difficulties people experience. Within the gambit of these approaches we can include three specific models which are widely used in social work: crisis intervention (Roberts 2000), task-centred work (Doel and Marsh 1992) and cognitive-behavioural therapy (Sheldon 1995).

- *Crisis intervention:* this approach adopts the view that a crisis is a kind of interruption to the normal, steady state of everyday life. A crisis is something which knocks people off balance because its demands exceed the normal range of resources we normally use to deal with the ups and downs of life. Interventions aim to help people identify the cause of the crisis, work through the feelings associated with it, obtain support during the crisis period and to think about and develop strategies to respond to the situation as positively as possible.

- *Task-centred work:* this approach responds to particular issues which are seen as problematic to the individual. It aims to prioritise particular issues and generate specific action plans to address them in collaboration with the person. Both worker and client may agree to undertake specific tasks until the difficulty is resolved.

- *Cognitive-behavioural therapy:* this approach utilises a range of social and behavioural learning techniques in conjunction with an understanding of how people think about and perceive certain things. By identifying what it is that makes someone anxious, for example, strategies can be developed to change the behaviour normally associated with those situations. By utilising the principles of learning theory, gentle and gradual exposure to social situations which the person learns to cope with are positively reinforced. This leads to the person feeling more confident and less anxious about these things and therefore begins to alter the way they think (cognition) about them.

Systems approaches

Systems theory (Goldstein 1973; Pincus and Minahan 1973) holds that individuals are part of other systems (families), which in their turn are part of wider systems (extended family), which in their turn form part of a bigger system (the community), and so on. These systems interact with each other in many complex ways and therefore have influence over each other. The original systems approaches were used in the biological sciences to explain the interrelationships between the different parts of the body to each other. The phrase 'the whole is more than the sum of its parts' is useful in understanding this approach. Latterly, systemic approaches have evolved to incorporate other theoretical perspectives, including ecology. Ecological systems theories are now quite common. These hold that all systems must relate to the wider social forces around them, including all forms of structural inequality, racism and other forms of oppression. This approach seeks to recognise these broader issues and incorporate them into its framework.

One form of this theory is presented by Germain and Gitterman (1980, 1996) as the 'life model' which is applicable to a range of social work settings. The model sees people very much as interdependent with each other and their environments, reacting and interacting constantly. The aim of the model is to increase the degree of fit between people and environments. Another application of a broad-based ecological systems theory is that represented in the Framework for Assessment of Children in Need and their Families (Department of Health 2000) and the 'My World' model (Scottish Executive 2005d). This framework draws upon the work of Bronfenbrenner (1979) and encourages practitioners to take an ecological approach to their assessment, seeing the child in relation to the wider systems which surround and affect them (see Figure 3.4) (Horwarth 2001; Jack 2000; Parker and Bradley 2003).

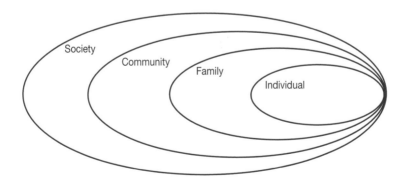

This model enables us to understand and examine the (inter) relationships between different systems of support. At each level there are supports available, although these may be more or less evident and effective.

Figure 3.4 *An ecological model of support*

This approach has been adopted and adapted for use in Scotland and is part of the move to develop an effective system concerned with assessment and information sharing. The Integrated Assessment Framework (IAF) incorporates the assessment triangle, as seen in Figure 3.5.

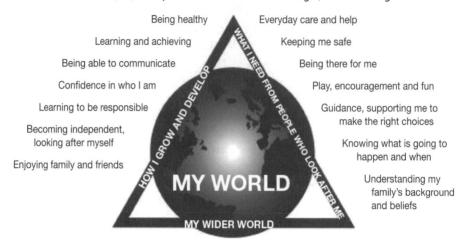

Support from family, friends and other people, School, Enough money, Work opportunities for my family, Local resources, Comfortable and safe housing, Belonging

Figure 3.5 *'My World'*

Source: Scottish Executive (2005d, p13)
Reproduced under the terms of Crown Copyright Policy Guidance Issued by HMSO.

The psychodynamic, psychological and systems approaches can all be utilised to provide support to individuals, families and groups. Used individually, they can offer solutions to some difficulties whilst perhaps not being able to address them all. Used together, however, and the potential is increased significantly (Figure 3.6). All of these approaches do have their pure forms, but if they are used creatively and used to inform each other, a practitioner can address many problems faced by clients. Do not be afraid to use them all if the situation appears to demand it. As we shall see below, the situation regarding Nikki is one where a range of approaches can be most beneficial.

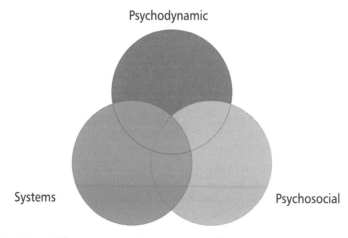

Figure 3.6 *Applying different approaches concurrently*

ACTIVITY 3.2

Nikki is 24, white Scottish with two children, Marcus, aged 8, and Mary, aged 4. The family live in a fifth-floor, two-bedroomed flat in a rather run-down part of the town with no family close by. The children's father Adam is of African descent. He left the family home a few weeks ago. He says he does not want to see the children anymore. Nikki's family live several hundred miles away and rarely visit or contact their daughter or grandchildren, having been very upset when Nikki told them that the children's father was black.

Nikki was sexually abused by her paternal uncle from the ages of 5 to 11 years old; she told her mum but she did not believe her. During her school years, Nikki spent lengthy periods of time playing truant from school as she found the work difficult. During this period she spent some time in a residential children's home.

At the age of 16 Nikki left her family home and stayed with a friend and her family, where she met Adam. She fell pregnant very soon after this. Since Adam left the family, Nikki has found it increasingly difficult to cope on her own. She receives no financial support from him and is unable to work because she has no childcare arrangements. Money is in short supply and because she has no transport, Nikki cannot shop at the large supermarket, relying instead upon the local shop for the family's groceries.

Nikki does not go out very much, finding the demands of single parenthood challenging. She has recently had a fall-out with her neighbour who has said that the children are noisy at nights. There are very few play areas nearby which Nikki feels are safe. Her friend Joanne has recently moved to the other side of the town with her new boyfriend so Nikki is feeling a little isolated.

Marcus attends the local primary school. He is doing quite well in his schoolwork although lately he has not been sleeping well. He says the other boys call him names and say nasty things about his dad. Nikki has begun to shout at her children a lot lately because what her neighbour said to her has worried her; she thinks she will be reported to the housing department and evicted.

The health visitor refers Nikki and the family to the social work department after Nikki tells her that she cannot cope anymore. You are allocated the case. How might you approach this situation?

Comment

At your first meeting, you would explain why you were there, who referred the family and why. This would offer Nikki a chance to discuss this with you. Open and honest communication is essential.

On the basis of the information referred to above there are a number of themes and issues which present themselves. Firstly, the situation at home seems to be getting fraught. The pressures of caring for two young children on a limited income and living five floors up are beginning to show. Your presence there is in response to a crisis; you spend some time with Nikki identifying the sources of stress and decide that she needs some support (welfare of the child, and psychosocial: crisis intervention). You might agree with Nikki that it would be a good idea to provide a family support worker one afternoon per week to take the family shopping to the large supermarket (psychosocial: task-centred). You might also agree to help Nikki access a pre-school place for Mary and ask the local Sure Start worker to visit Nikki to discuss other practical and emotional support she might find useful (psychosocial: task-centred, and systems approach: local community systems).

In relation to how Nikki is feeling about the current situation, you might arrange to spend some time with her discussing this and suggesting ways in which she might deal with her anxiety about going out to the park with the children (psychosocial: cognitive-behavioural). You might also begin to speak with Nikki about her feelings around the abuse she suffered at the hands of her uncle (psychotherapeutic: counselling) or arrange for someone else to do this longer-term piece of work (inter-agency collaboration).

In terms of Nikki's social isolation, you might offer a place at the local family centre where she might take Mary a couple of mornings per week (psychosocial: task-centred, and systems approach: community systems). This might be a source of support to Nikki in relation to her parenting skills which she perhaps feels are lacking. As Nikki begins to feel more confident about her role as a mum and as an individual in her own right (psychosocial: cognitive-behavioural approach), you might encourage her to contact her parents and try and regain their support (systems approach: family networks) and/or that of Adam. Contact with the children's father may help Marcus feel better about himself (psychosocial: task-centred, and systems approach: family systems) and school (systems approach: community systems). Nikki may well develop her confidence much more, particularly as she sees Marcus settling back into school and sleeping better, and Mary enjoying her time at the pre-school group and family centre. Nikki may look towards enrolling on a college course in the future to get more qualifications and get a good job once Mary begins school.

C H A P T E R   S U M M A R Y

Working with children, young people and their families is a challenging but rewarding experience. This chapter has looked at a broad range of factors which need to be considered, including the need to have reference to the practice context, an awareness of your own abilities and an understanding of the theoretical perspectives you might apply to assist you in your work, along with a knowledge of some of the initiatives currently ongoing in Scotland.

The following texts are suggested as excellent source material to expand upon some of the issues in this chapter.

Payne, **M** (2005) *Modern social work theory (3rd edition)*. Basingstoke: Palgrave Macmillan.

An excellent source book on social work theory and something of a modern classic.

Healy, **K** (2005) *Social work theories in context: creating frameworks for practice*. Basingstoke: Palgrave Macmillan.

Another excellent text which links theory and practice very effectively. Well written.

www.scotland.gov.uk/Topics/People/Young-People The website of the Scottish Executive with the focus on young people. Follow the links.

Chapter 4
Child protection

Introduction

Child protection is one set of practices through which relations between families and the state are constituted and regulated. This set of practices enables us to examine the negotiation of the relationship between public and private life. Modern management of the legal, social and cultural boundaries between families and the state is effected by the mobilisation of a range of professional forms of knowledge and practice such as law, medicine, psychology and social work, specialising in determining where and when intervention is reasonable and legitimate, all of which are premised on the idea of the 'best interests of the child. (Ashenden 2004, p10).

The protection of children from abuse and neglect is an integral part of the work of the social worker and other professionals and agencies, although social work is the key statutory agency with responsibility for this (see for example section 53 Children (S) Act 1995).

In this chapter we shall look at the current legal and policy context of this aspect of social work and consider this in relation to the broader issues of ethically sound practice.

What do we mean by child abuse and neglect?

Giving a proper name to an entity can often make it seem more substantial or more unified than it actually is… (Garland 1990, p1).

The first thing to say is that child abuse and neglect are socially constructed. This means that our understanding of what constitutes abusive and/or neglectful behaviour is subject to change and redefinition depending on the (historical) time we live in and the physical place we inhabit, which makes this whole area one which is culturally and historically relative. We also have to consider the moral dimension. What is considered to be abusive by one person may not be seen as such by another. The debate concerning corporal punishment is one example of this (Scottish Executive 2002c), as is the situation of children used in factory work in Victorian times (see Fraser 2003; Ferguson 2004; and any of Charles Dickens' works for commentary upon such things). Thus, what constitutes child abuse and neglect is also based upon value judgements and it is often the case that the views of powerful interest groups take precedence. We need therefore to consider who it is that defines these things and to be aware that legal definitions of child abuse are those which tend to represent the views of those powerful groups.

The World Health Organisation provides a general definition of child abuse:

Child abuse or maltreatment constitutes all forms of physical and/or emotional ill treatment, sexual abuse, neglect or negligent treatment or commercial or other exploitation, resulting in actual or potential harm in the child's health, survival, development or dignity in the context of a relationship of responsibility, trust or power. (Scottish Executive 2002d, p6).

This definition is very wide and can be applied at a number of levels (the individual, the family, the community or society) in relation to who might be responsible for the abuse or maltreatment, which in and of itself is not specifically defined nor delineated.

At a more specific level, the Scottish Office (as it was then called) produced a general definition of abuse along with distinct categorisations for the purposes of effecting the registration of those children who had suffered or were at risk of suffering some form of abuse or neglect:

> *Children may be in need of protection where their basic needs are not being met, in a manner appropriate to their stage of development, and they will be at risk from avoidable acts of commission or omission on the part of their parent(s), sibling(s) or other relative(s), or a carer (i.e. the person(s) while not a parent who has actual custody of a child). (Scottish Office 1998, Annex C, and Scottish Executive 2002d, p7).*

RESEARCH SUMMARY

Risk

Within social work generally and particularly in social work with children, young people and their families there is an emphasis on the identification, assessment and management of risk (Brearley 1982; Cooper 2003; Dalgleish 2003; Department of Health 1988; Ferguson 1997, 2004; Hagell 1998; Lupton 1999; Moore 1996; Samra-Tibbets and Raynes 1999). The likelihood of harm befalling a child in any given situation is something which has to be considered as an integral part to any assessment and within any intervention. The assessment of risk and its subsequent management should be seen as a normative part of good practice and it is important for you to appreciate that risk assessment is something you do every day in every encounter you have, both personally and professionally. It is important that you approach risk assessment and management in an integrated way.

What is risk? According to the formal definitions, risk is the relative variation in possible outcomes based on measures of probability. It is also something very complex, fluid, subjective, interpretative, interdependent and uncertain; in short, it is messy. These two definitions complement each other quite well. The first gives us a somewhat formal and technical-rational view whilst the second locates the whole issue in the realm of the subjective experiences of the individual(s) involved.

Whether a child is likely to be harmed is a judgement about possible future events based upon knowledge of the current situation and past actions/events which may be of relevance. What is required is an objective measure of the level of risk which can be given with a particular degree of certainty. Neither of these things exists. What does exist, however, are ways of thinking about the potential for harm in any given situation and indicators we can look for which can increase our predictive power. These exist in the form of checklists and other assessment tools which have pulled together details of those factors which are more likely to indicate some degree of risk if they are present in a situation than if they are not. For example, data would suggest that where there is a history of family violence, a history of abuse and neglect, young parents, mental health problems, disabilities, poor attachment relationships and substance misuse issues, then there is a greater likelihood of harm befalling a child in this situation than in one where none of these factors appears to exist (Browne and Saqi 1988). This is not to say, however, that harm will befall a child; rather that these factors indicate a situation where there are a greater number of potential stressors which may act as triggers to precipitate an abusive

Continued

act. Similarly, in situations where there were none of those factors present, we cannot rule out the possibility of a child being harmed. We just do not know. We cannot predict with 100% accuracy; the only thing you can be certain of is that this whole area is uncertain.

Risk assessment involves the identification of potential risk factors (like those mentioned above) and working out how these might be managed. If a child is living in a situation similar to that described above, you would have to consider what strengths there are in the situation which may offset the potential risks. Brearley (1982) refers to hazards and dangers; hazards are those factors which either introduce or increase the possibility of an undesired outcome whilst danger *refers to the feared outcome itself. These may reside in individuals or within the environment or within a situation generally.*

Risk assessment and management is not an exact science, despite what people may lead you to believe. Good, reflective, ethically sound social work practice should allow for an approach to risk which is integrated, realistic and proportional. You should record your observations and decisions clearly and utilise your colleagues and other personnel in any assessment.

Categorising abuse and neglect

There are five specific categories of child abuse which are used to locate a child's name on the Child Protection Register. This register is held by the local authority and is a list of the names of all those children who have been abused or neglected or who it is thought are at risk of such abuse and neglect in a particular local authority area and who have been through the child protection process (see Figure 4.1 later in this chapter). These registers were introduced in the mid-1970s following the public inquiry into the death of Maria Colwell, who was killed by her step-father (Department of Health and Social Security 1974a). The resulting public inquiry, amongst other things, resulted in the issuing of circular LASSL (74) (13) (Department of Health and Social Security 1974b), which triggered the establishment of what we now refer to as the child protection system. This included the development of Area Review Committees (now Area Child Protection Committees (Scottish Executive 2005e)) and through these, child protection conferences and the Child Protection Register. These registers are held by the local authority and through a strict access protocol are accessible by other agencies who, if they have concerns about a child, can check to see whether their name is on the register. For example, medical/nursing staff in a casualty department may be presented with a child who has an injury, the explanation for which may be inconsistent with what is being seen. If the child's name is found to be on the register, then a more detailed investigation into the situation may be called for as there is clearly a history of previous concern and the child is already the subject of an inter-agency protection plan.

The following are the main categories against which children's names might be placed on the Child Protection Register and are the operational definitions used by all local authorities in Scotland at this time.

Physical abuse (also referred to as non-accidental injury or NAI): 'actual or attempted physical injury to a child under the age of 16 where there is definite knowledge, or reasonable suspicion, that the injury was inflicted or knowingly not prevented'.

Sexual abuse: 'Any child below the age of 16 may be deemed to have been sexually abused when any person(s) by design or neglect, exploits the child, directly or indirectly, in any activity intended to lead to the sexual arousal or other forms of gratification of that person or any other person(s) including organised networks. This definition holds whether or not there has been genital contact and whether or not the child is said to have initiated the behaviour.'

Non-organic failure to thrive: 'Children who significantly fail to reach normal growth and developmental milestones (i.e. physical growth, weight, motor, social and intellectual development) where physical and genetic reasons have been medically eliminated and a diagnosis of failure to thrive has been established.'

Emotional abuse: 'Failure to provide for the child's basic emotional needs such as to have a severe effect on the behaviour and development of the child.'

Physical neglect: 'When a child's essential needs are not met and this is likely to cause impairment to physical health and development. Such needs include food, clothing, clean-liness, shelter and warmth. A lack of appropriate care results in persistent or severe exposure, through negligence to circumstances which endanger the child.'

(Scottish Executive 2002d, pp7–8).

There are a number of other types of abuse which have been identified and generally fall as subsets of the above categories or arise as a result of the above categorisations being clustered together. These are noted as including:

- organised abuse
- child prostitution
- child pornography
- ritual abuse
- institutional abuse
- factitious illness (Munchausen's syndrome by proxy)
- domestic abuse
- foetal abuse
- substance misuse
- racial abuse
- female genital mutilation
- forced marriage
- children who harm themselves
- children who run away
- medical neglect

- animal abuse

- system abuse.

(Scottish Executive 2002d, pp9–19).

These formulations of child abuse represent how thinking about the subject has developed over the past few years. As more knowledge becomes available, more situations can be defined as being abusive.

RESEARCH SUMMARY

The organisational arrangements for the protection of children were instigated on a large scale in 1974, as we saw above. Since that time these arrangements have grown in both size and complexity and have often evolved in response to other tragedies. It cannot be denied that the presence of these inter-agency arrangements has been successful in protecting many children. It is also true that a number of children have not been protected despite being known to social work and other agencies and having their name on the Child Protection Register (Reder et al. 1993). In Scotland, the report following the death of Kennedy McFarlane at the hands of her step-father in 1999 recommended that there be a review of child protection arrangements across Scotland (Hammond 2001). This led to a review and audit of child protection services across Scotland and the resulting report, 'It's everyone's job to make sure I'm alright' (Scottish Executive 2002e) made commentary on a number of themes and issues as well as making a number of recommendations (Daniel 2004). These included:

- *that all agencies should review their child protection procedures;*

- *that standards of practice be developed and that all agencies should in future review all services against these;*

- *that the remit of Child Protection Committees should be reviewed;*

- *current arrangements for the development and dissemination of knowledge about child abuse and neglect should be strengthened;*

- *a long-term study on the effectiveness of current methods of intervention in relation to child abuse and neglect should begin;*

- *a single shared assessment format should be developed in conjunction with computer-based information systems;*

- *minimum standards of professional knowledge and competence should be developed in relation to those professionals undertaking work in this area.*

(Scottish Executive 2002e, pp13–16)

As well as producing a report, the audit and review also commissioned a literature review, which provides an overview on current issues in child abuse and neglect and child protection (Scottish Executive 2002d).

Theories of and perspectives on child abuse and neglect

In order to appreciate some of the realities of child protection work it is important for you to understand some of the theories and explanations put forward to try to explain why some people abuse and neglect (their) children. According to Corby (2000), there appear to be three main categories of theories of causation. These are psychological, social psychological and sociological. I shall adopt this categorisation here although it is important to appreciate that these are areas which can overlap quite significantly.

Psychological theories

As we saw in Chapter 3, the discourse of psychology is very powerful within social work and has contributed much to the formulation and development of descriptive and explanatory accounts of human behaviour.

Within the range of these theories are a number of approaches and perspectives. These include attachment theory (Crittenden 1999; Howe 2005), learning theory (Bee and Boyd 2003; Skinner 1980), psychodynamic theories (Freud 1991) and cognitive theories (Eysenck and Keane 2005; Piaget and Inhelder 1969). The main emphasis of these theories is that the causatory mechanism of and for the abuse is located within the individual themselves. It is intra-personal.

The assumptions within these theories and models of causation see individual pathology as a key determining factor. For example, it may be that the individual had themselves been abused as a child and therefore feels that to do this to their child is in fact the norm based on their own prior experiences (learning theory). Similarly, if the adult–child attachment relationship has been disrupted in some way, the parent may have no feelings for the child and could therefore abuse them or allow them to be abused by others without worrying about this. If a child has had very negative early life experiences and did not form any significant attachments to other people, when they grow up they may have a range of emotional problems which mean they cannot respond appropriately to their child's needs (attachment theory) (Bacon and Richardson 2001; Crittenden and Ainsworth 1989; Egeland and Sroufe 1981). It may also be the case that the parent feels compelled to behave in certain ways in order to assuage their own feelings of inadequacy or guilt. For example, they may feel that a crying child is a symptom of their own failure to be an effective parent, so may abuse the child whilst trying to keep them quiet (psychodynamic theory). Parents may also think and process information in particular ways which may result in abuse (Klahr 1992; Crittenden 1993). If a child cries a lot the parent may well feel that they are doing it deliberately to 'wind them up'; this is called an *attribution bias* and can affect how we interpret incoming information as we may attribute certain characteristics to the child which are, in reality, not present. If this is the case, then the child may be blamed for their own abuse and if the crying stops when they abuse the child, this may act as reinforcement for the persons actions, so they do it again.

Social psychological theories

The emphasis within these theories and perspectives is that of the inter-personal. These accounts acknowledge the influence of broader social factors which operate within the family and society as a whole and affect the individual. There is a rich literature concerning the impact that group dynamics have on the individual in the form of influence, pressure, persuasion and conformity (Barron et al. 2006). These ideas can be seen to operate within the (group) setting of the family. In some situations one parent may feel compelled to behave towards the child in a particular way because the other more powerful parent behaves in this way or there are other pressures from outside the family. These kinds of situation can be seen in families where domestic and other forms of violence are present (Mullender et al. 2002). Other perspectives include social learning theory (Bandura 1977). This theory is a development from traditional learning theory (operant conditioning) which takes account of cognitive factors in relation to observed behaviours. For example, a person may see someone doing something and although they themselves do not receive any reward or reinforcement (as in learning theory), they see the behaviour as having some kind of positive outcome for the other person (a child stops crying, for example). They may adopt this as a mode of behaving if they feel it might be of use to them.

Sociological theories

There are a number of perspectives within the realm of sociology which have been applied to discussions of child abuse. These theories and perspectives seek to explain the uniquely social origins and consequences of individual and group behaviour (Giddens 2001; Haralambos and Holborn 2004). These approaches have as their focus the macro perspective which embraces the impact of wider social, structural and cultural factors upon individuals. As Healy points out, 'Sociological discourse asserts that humans are profoundly social beings. It challenges individualistic explanations of social and personal problems by drawing attention to the social practices and social structures that sustain these problems' (2005, p59). These sociological contributions are concerned with the relevance of social structures, economics, class, gender and race and how differing inequalities emerge which may contribute to the actions of individuals in certain circumstances. Sociological discourse would also comment upon the presence of certain cultural practices (for example, child rearing) which may involve aspects of power, the cultural sanctioning or otherwise of certain social acts and the creation and legitimation of certain social institutions which may 'police' certain individuals and certain culturally specific behaviours (Ashenden 2004; Foucault 1991).

These approaches incorporate analyses from a number of differing perspectives, including feminism (Dominelli 2002), Marxism (Fook 2002), post-modernism (Healy 2000) and children's rights (Freeman 1983; Goldstein *et al.* 1979). All of these aim to offer some level of explanation to account for child abuse and neglect focusing on the contribution of wider social forces to these situations whilst delimiting the impact of individual pathology as a causal factor.

Integrative approaches

In addition to the three groupings referred to above, there is a fourth, which I feel offers a more integrated perspective upon some of these issues.

The Russian psychologist and semiotician Lev Vygotsky (1978) developed a theory of human development which is referred to as socio-historical or socio-cultural. The theory takes a broadly Marxist approach to its analysis and offers an account of human growth and development in relation to the social and cultural activities of any given society at any given point in time. Vygotskyian theory says that as both children and adults we learn and develop complex forms of thinking through social interactions rather than just through our own explorations, as Piagetian theory would suggest, or through simple reinforcement mechanisms, as behaviourism would argue. The theory offers the potential to explain why people might develop particular patterns of thinking and behaving which are inherently abusive or damaging but seen to be normative by that individual and which might therefore be resistant to change. In this regard there is considerable importance attached to the role of the person's own emotional experiences as a vehicle through which development takes place in the way that it does. The theory integrates elements of social learning theory and psychodynamic theory into a framework which can account for the development of thought, language and action.

The work of Bronfenbrenner (1979, 1986) has recently undergone something of a renaissance. His ecological theory of human development explains the nature of ontogenesis (development) in terms of the relationships between people and their environments or their contexts. This account of development sees individuals responding and reacting to a range of forces at a number of different levels, all of which influence how we think, feel and ultimately act (see Crawford and Walker 2003).

Another related approach is that developed by Lewin (1997), who refers to the 'life space' or 'total situation' of a person. In this formulation, human development and behaviour are seen as products of the total situation of a person, which includes personal psychology and the environment.

There are a number of similarities between these perspectives upon development. Each of them argues that individual development is a function of both intra- and interpersonal factors which are affected by the environment(s) within which individuals function and live out their lives. Lewin emphasised the importance of considering the interplay between the psychological and geographical (physical) environments whilst Vygotsky focused upon the role of emotional experience as a mediating influence upon development. Bronfenbrenner is more explicit about the effects of wider system variables upon human development and, like Vygotsky, sees the phenomenological or subjective experience of an individual as being a key factor in determining developmental outcomes. In this way, these subjective interpretations can account for why individuals living in similar circumstances may develop and behave very differently.

All of these approaches have something to offer in terms of helping practitioners to understand why child abuse and neglect may occur. It is important for you to be eclectic in your thinking about these matters and to be open to new developments and strands of thought throughout your career. This is the reflective and reflexive practitioner. All of the theories and approaches referred to can offer only a partial explanation; some may be more relevant than others to particular individuals but overall there are elements from each which can be usefully adopted to assist in trying to understand these things.

The framework for child protection in Scotland

The protection of children takes place within a particular legislative and policy framework which has grown quite substantially over the past few years. Table 4.1 lists the main components as well as other key sources of information.

Table 4.1 The framework for child protection in Scotland

- The Social Work (S) Act 1968 (s12)
- Education (S) Act 1980
- Foster Children (S) Act 1984
- Age of Legal Capacity (S) Act 1991
- Children (S) Act 1995 (especially Part 2)
- *Scotland's Children. The Children (Scotland) Act 1995 Regulations and Guidance: Volumes 1–4* (Scottish Office 1997a, b, c, d)
- The Emergency Child Protection Measures (S) Regulations 1996
- Housing (S) Act 1997
- Police (S) Act 1997
- *Child Protection: A Shared Responsibility*. There are also separate guidelines for health and education professionals (Scottish Office 1998).
- Data Protection Act 1998
- Human Rights Act 1998
- *For Scotland's children: better integrated children's services* (Scottish Executive 2001a)
- *It's everyone's job to make sure I'm alright*. Report of the Child Protection Audit and Review (Scottish Executive 2002e)
- *Getting our priorities right* (Scottish Executive 2003c)
- Protection of children (S) Act 2003
- Anti-Social Behaviour etc. (S) Act 2004
- *Protecting children and young people: the charter* (Scottish Executive 2004c)
- *Protecting children and young people: framework for standards* (Scottish Executive 2004d)
- Guidance on Child Protection Committees (2005)
- UNCHR/UNCRC
- *Local inter-agency guidelines* (issued through child protection committees)
- *Local single-agency guidelines* (social work, police, health and education)]

Responding to child abuse and neglect

At one level, the whole area of dealing with child abuse and neglect is a highly regulated and formalised state activity with formal mechanisms (broadly referred to as 'child protection proce-dures') in place, underpinned by legislation to be adhered to by all social workers, particularly those with statutory responsibilities. On the other hand, dealing with a child who has been abused or neglected, whose parents may deny any involvement in this and who are angry and frightened is a very personal, 'in your face' experience which is fluid, subjective, messy, noisy and scary; something very difficult to regulate. Ferguson (2004) describes it like this:

> It is thus an experience of power and control, but equally of caring and compassion: of helping and tending for others, of relieving the suffering of children and often their parents and other carers, many of whom no one else wants to know: of talking, listening, group meetings and often boring bureaucratic routine: of being blamed for the deaths of children or in other ways getting it wrong, and being made accountable and subjected to managerial guidance and control. It is pervasively an experience of mobility, of acting at speed to reach children, of the emotions and senses and intimate engagement with the sights, sounds and smells of other's lives and homes, their tragedy and pain, which threatens to become the worker's own: of pervasive anxiety, risk, danger and despair, but some joy and laughs too. (Ferguson 2004, p1)

These differing perspectives are sometimes seen in discrete terms. The regulatory mecha-nisms which exist are there for all to see; they are objective and as a social worker you are expected to know what these are and know when and how to use them. There is a clear, bureaucratic process to be followed (Weber 1946). According to Howe (1992), the many child abuse inquiries which have taken place have resulted in the growth of policies and procedures designed to make the protection of children more prescriptive and therefore more manageable. The face-to-face encounter between you and the child and the family is, however, one where all the rules become fluid. Conflict at some level is inevitable. All is subjective. Your efforts to enforce the law, the regulations and to follow the guidance issued by the state and your agency are subject to interpretation in the heat of the moment. Feelings on all sides become intense and you have to interpret what you see, hear, smell, touch and feel accurately because if you don't, you run the risk of getting it wrong with (potentially) dire consequences on all sides: at best you offend the family, at worst you fail to prevent a child being abused and/or neglected. These are the differing and sometimes competing elements of child protection work.

The child protection process

Firstly we shall consider the structure and function of the current child protection system and look at the processes and procedures which currently exist. Figure 4.1 represents this.

Following the receipt of information to the effect that there are concerns about the safety or welfare of a child or young person, there are a number of tasks which need to be undertaken immediately. These are to establish the facts concerning the circumstances which have given rise to the suspicions and then to decide whether there are in fact grounds for concern. This would necessitate making contact with the referrer and other relevant agencies, particular school staff, health personnel (GP, health visitor) and anyone else who may be in a position to offer information. These initial checks are designed to screen out those referrals which are perhaps more appropriately dealt with in other ways rather than by reference to child protection procedures.

CASE STUDY

A referral is made to your office alleging that Graham, aged 3, is being abused by his mother. You are told that his mother regularly hits and shouts at him and does not feed him properly. You contact the local health centre to find out who Graham's GP and health visitor are. Upon speaking to both of them you are told that Graham has been seen by the health visitor regularly and that he has also recently been seen by the GP for a chest infection. Neither of these professionals has any concerns over his safety or welfare. You are told that he is reaching all his normal developmental milestones and there are no concerns over his growth. You decide to visit the family with the health visitor to assess the situation. Your inquiry reveals that Sally, Graham's mum, lives alone and is struggling with the care of her toddler son. She has been finding things a little difficult lately because Graham has been ill with a chest infection. There are no signs of any injuries and the quality of the interactions between Graham and his mum appear to be good. Both the GP and the health visitor have seen him naked at the surgery, so can vouch that they have seen no evidence to support this claim. In discussing the referral with Sally it is agreed that some form of family-based support would be appropriate as well as a referral to the local family centre where Sally and Graham can be involved in a parenting group and other activities.

CHILD PROTECTION PROCESS FLOWCHART

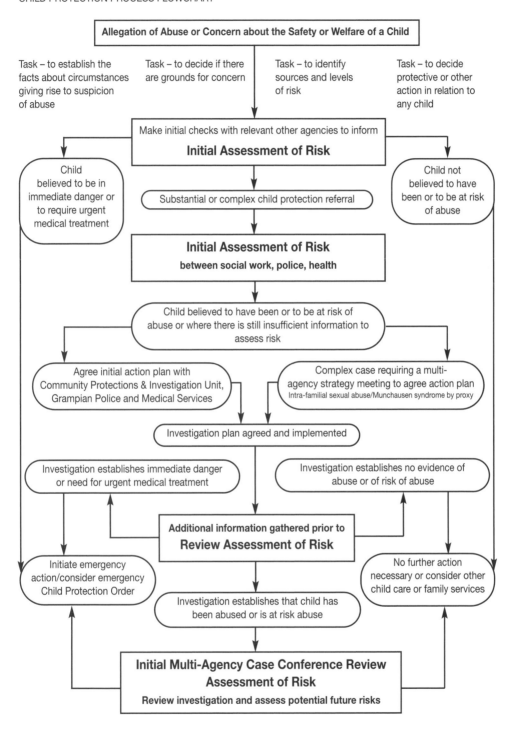

Figure 4.1 *Child protection process*

Reproduced with kind permission from the North East of Scotland Child Protection Committee Guidelines (p43). Available at www.nescpc.org.uk/nescpc/CPguidelines.pdf

Comment

This is an example of initial inquiries being undertaken which reveal a situation requiring support. The initial checks and the visit to the family provided information concerning the perceived level of risk to the child. On the basis of these inquiries a particular course of action was followed which seemed appropriate. It could also have been the case that no support was required. Everyone struggles sometimes and if the mother had had other supports around her (family or friends), then it is conceivable that no further action would have been an appropriate course to take. This particular situation is one which we can use to think about how situations are defined.

In the 1990s childcare social work went through a period known as the *re-focusing debate*. Child protection services had been the subject of many criticisms not just because of tragedies which had taken place but also because of the way in which families were seen to be treated within the child protection system *per se*. The publication of *Child protection: messages from research* (Department of Health 1995) highlighted the way in which social work services seemed to be dominated by an approach which focused upon (child) protection rather than need. It was argued that because of this particular orientation many children who were in need did not receive a service (Aldgate and Tunstill 1995). Local authorities argued that this apparent concern with protection reflected the need to target scarce resources. However, contemporary research argued that the child protection system was ineffective as a means of targeting these resources (Farmer and Owen 1995; Thorburn et al. 1995). Prior to this debate, the above situation may well have resulted in no service being offered at all simply because there were no immediate child protection concerns in evidence following the initial investigation. This approach therefore recognises the false economy of not responding to children and families in need of support. The need for support, if not acknowledged, may well develop into a need for protection which serves no useful purpose for anyone.

In any situation where information is received which suggests a child or young person may be at risk or in danger, prompt action is essential. Any referral must be dealt with as a priority. In all circumstances it is important to try to obtain as much information as possible from the referrer, including their name and contact details. Some referrals can be made anonymously and there are a number of reasons for this being the case, although in the majority of cases referrers are happy to give details so that you (or colleagues) can get back to them to discuss things in more detail later if required. When referrers do give details their identity is usually not disclosed to the family.

Where initial checks appear to support a view that a child or young person may be at immediate risk or in danger, emergency procedures may need to be considered. These could include an application for a Child Protection Order under section 57 or an application for emergency authorisation to remove a child under section 61 of the Children (S) Act 1995.

Applying for a Child Protection Order

Applying for a Child Protection Order is not done lightly and represents the end point of a continuum of concern where it is believed that removing a child from his or her parents or carers is the only way to ensure the child is safe. This step should only be taken after efforts to secure the cooperation of parents/carers have proved to be ineffective or have been ruled out, and other means to secure the child's protection (for example, being cared for by other family members or friends whilst enquiries continue) have been discounted (McGhee and Francis 2003). Sections 57–60 of the 1995 Act refer to the grounds, processes and procedures relevant to this course of action. Local area guidelines, usually issued by the appropriate Area Child Protection Committee, should also be consulted as well as agency guidance relevant to the local setting. The flowchart in Figure 4.2 illustrates the process of applying for and implementing a Child Protection Order.

CASE STUDY

You receive information from the local primary school to the effect that Sam, aged 7, has been discovered to have severe bruising to his back, arms and legs. Initial checks with health personnel reveal a recent history of missed appointments for Sam's younger sister as well as missed ante-natal appointments for the mother. Inquiries with the local police reveal that there have been reports from neighbours recently of disturbances at the house late at night although their inquiries revealed nothing of substance. Upon meeting Sam you note that the bruising is very significant and you refer the matter to the police child protection unit. Contact with the family results in hostility from the father and a refusal to allow you into the house to see Sam's sister (aged 4) and to discuss the bruising to Sam. You note that the mother has a black eye. Attempts to discuss the situation are met with aggression even with a police presence. You are aware that there are no other family members in the area. In consultation with the police, legal services and colleagues, it is agreed that the best course of action is to apply for Child Protection Orders in relation to both children and to place them in foster care.

Comment

In a situation like this where attempts have been made to engage with the family with little or no success and where tensions are rising, removal of the children is a possible course of action. This would ensure their safety whilst the situation is investigated more fully. The Child Protection Order would allow Sam to be medically examined and treated as well as ensuring he is safe. The order in relation to the younger child would allow access to her even in the face of parental opposition and again guarantee her safety. Even though you had no actual evidence that the younger child had been harmed, the injuries to Sam (for which there was no explanation) were significant enough to warrant concern for her safety. The application would be considered by the Sheriff.

The reaction of the father all point to significant risk. Following the removal of the children, the matter would be referred to the Reporter to the children's hearing and a multi-agency case conference would be convened. There are a number of strict rules which apply to the application for and the implementation and review of CPOs (see McNorrie 2005, pp226–53).

The child protection case conference

Where there are concerns about the safety or well-being of a child, it may be necessary to convene a multi-agency child protection case conference. This would take place once initial inquiries are completed and offers a forum within which information concerning a child and their family is shared. The child's needs and requirements will be considered and those services and agencies felt to be able to offer a service identified. A multi-agency child protection plan will be drawn up in consultation with the child (if appropriate) and the family and should identify those actions deemed necessary to ensure the child's safety and well-being. The CP plan may recommend that a Child Protection Order be sought if the situation is considered to be serious enough, although it is usually the case that any emergency action will already been have taken. It is vitally important that the child (as appropriate) and their family are involved in the process, including conferences, from the outset. Much research has been undertaken on the child protection system and the findings are of great interest. Farmer and Owen (1995), Department of Health (1995) and Cleaver and Freeman (1995), for example, all pointed to those factors which made the convening of a conference more or less likely and more or less effective. The involvement of parents, carers and children within the child protection process has similarly been the subject of research (Bell 1999; Cleaver and Freeman 1996; Dale 2004; Thorburn et al. 1995).

The conference would also decide whether or not to place the child's name on the Child Protection Register under one or more of the categories referred to above. This is usually done at the initial child protection conference and the situation and the registration status of the child would be reconsidered at the review child protection conference (see Figure 4.3). Review conferences take place at intervals designed to reflect the level of ongoing concern surrounding a situation, but usually at six-monthly intervals or sooner if the situation warrants it.

CASE STUDY

You receive information from the school which suggests that Sally, aged 9, is having difficulties. Lately she appears to have become more and more withdrawn. Her school work is deteriorating and her attendance has begun to be a cause for concern. The school have spoken to her mum, who has been very cooperative but can shed no light on the situation. Your contact with the family reveals that the house is used as a meeting place for drug users. Your contact with Sally reveals little as she is unwilling to speak, although she did say that she was often cared for by 'Billy'. Your initial assessment suggests there are causes for concern, particularly around the physical state of the house and the presence of unknown individuals who seem to come and go as they please. A multi-agency strategy meeting is convened in order that information from all relevant agencies can be shared. On the basis of this an action plan is drawn up and further contact with the family undertaken. Further inquiries with the police reveal that 'Billy' has a previous conviction for a sexual offence against a child and he is therefore a Schedule 1 offender (Criminal Procedure (S) Act 1995: Schedule 1). This information leads to the convening of a multi-agency child protection case conference. On the basis of information presented to the conference, Sally's name is placed on the Child Protection Register under the category of being at risk of sexual abuse. A child protection plan is agreed upon and work is then undertaken with the family on a range of issues and a referral is made to the Reporter (s.52(2)b).

CHILD PROTECTION ORDERS – SECTIONS 57–60

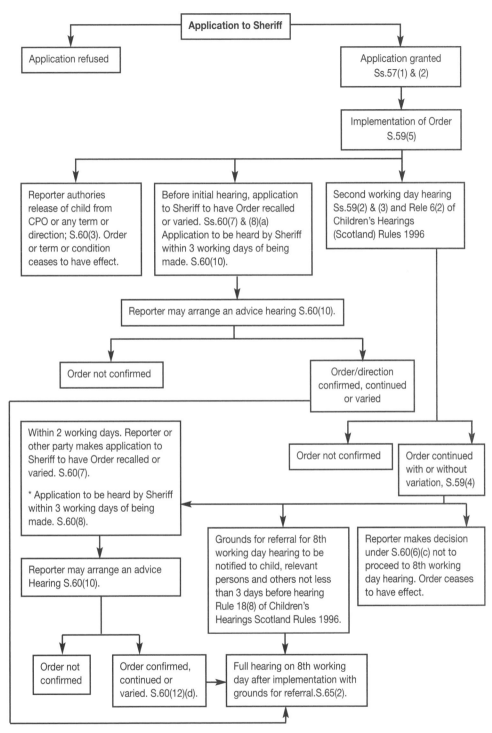

Figure 4.2 *Child Protection Orders*

Reproduced with kind permission from the North East of Scotland Child Protection Committee Guidelines (p100). Available at www.nescpc.org.uk/nescpc/CPguidelines.pdf

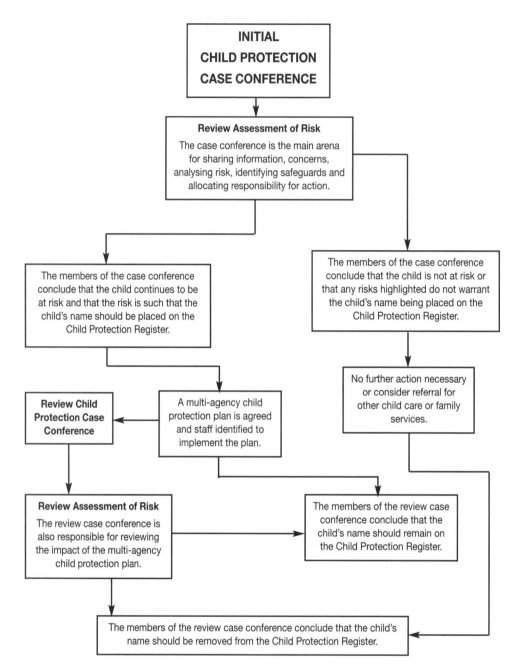

Figure 4.3 *Child protection case conference flowchart*

Reproduced with kind permission from the North East of Scotland Child Protection Committee Guidelines (p60). Available at www.nescpc.org.uk/nescpc/CPguidelines.pdf

Comment

Situations like Sally's present real challenges to the practitioner. The need for inter-agency cooperation is obvious and illustrates the capacity of such networks to provide information which can be used to inform decision-making. Where there are unsubstantiated accounts of harm to a child, the need is clearly for practitioners to consider the broader context and form judgements on the basis of available information. Risk assessment and subsequent decision-making are not an exact science; rather it is a process informed by knowledge, values, skills, time, place, space and context. According to Hollows (2003), citing Hammond (1987, 1996), there are a number of variables which affect our capacity to form judgements and which lead us to adopt strategies which are either more or less intuitive or analytical. The type of situation and the amount of available information are key factors in determining whether intuition is relied upon more than analysis in the heat of the moment. In the situation referred to above, judgements may well be made intuitively at the time, with the subsequent assessment processes contributing to an increase in available information which allows for a more rational and analytical approach to be adopted to inform longer-term decision-making. The CP case conference is one forum where shared decision-making takes place and whilst there are no statutory provisions relating to CP conferences, they are an integral and very important part of the child protection process and all local authorities in Scotland adopt this mechanism. However, there are suggestions that other mechanisms might be utilised to bring professionals and families together before the stage of a formal, multi-agency child protection conference is reached.

RESEARCH SUMMARY

Family Group Conferences (FGCs) have evolved from an approach adopted initially in New Zealand (McElrea 1998). Essentially, an FGC is a meeting between family members and other relevant people with an interest in a child's situation which aims to develop and provide workable solutions to identified problems. These might be concerns over a child's safety or worries about offending behaviour or anything really which has raised concern to a level where professional and/or statutory intervention is being considered (Brown 2003; Marsh and Crow 1997; Wilson and Bell 2001).

The philosophies of the approach incorporate a number of assumptions about the role of the family in caring for children and young people (Burford and Hudson 2000); the potential inherent within kinship care (Broad 2001; Ryburn 1998); the empowerment of children, young people and their families (Dalrymple and Horan 2003; Sieppert et al. 2000); and the role of professionals in the process.

An FGC is a meeting owned by the child and his or her family which is designed to focus on issues of concern. The view is that families have a deeper commitment to the process and the solutions if they are involved in these. The role of the professional is primarily one of facilitation. The conference would aim to generate solutions to problems and draw upon resources within the (extended) family system as well as those offered by professionals.

As a resource, the FGC model has some promise in terms of adding value to the whole process of addressing concerns about a child's safety and welfare. The FGC is not intended to replace current mechanisms for the protection of children but as an addition to this process it has potential, although it has yet to be seen how effective they are in relation to long-term outcomes (Sundell and Vinnerljung 2004).

How many children are abused and neglected in Scotland?

The statistics presented here represent only those children known to the authorities. These figures do not represent children who may be being abused and neglected at this time but have not been identified.

Table 4.2 *Numbers of children referred, subject to a case conference, registered, de-registered and on Child Protection Registers 1999–2004*

	1999	2000	2001	2002	2003	2004
Referrals	7310	7201	6619	7172	8033	8366
Case conferences	2734	2593	2352	2851	3244	3351
Registrations	1962	1890	1783	1979	2517	2440
De-registrations	1936	2112	1687	2216	2408	2634
Children on CP Registers	2361	2050	2000	2018	2289	2245

Source: www.scotland.gov.uk/stats/bulletins/00369-31.asp (accessed 04/07/05).

Table 4.3 *Children registered following a case conference 1999–2004: category of abuse/risk identified by conference*

	1999	2000	2001	2002	2003	2004
Physical injury	836	713	688	644	766	741
Sexual abuse	344	286	256	249	310	233
Emotional abuse	209	235	270	264	438	435
Physical abuse	563	639	558	809	969	1015
Other	10	18	11	13	33	16
Totals	1962	1890	1783	1979	2517	2440

Source: www.scotland.gov.uk/stats/bulletins/00369-28.asp (accessed 04/07/05).

Tables 4.2 and 4.3 offer an official indication of the size of the population of children abused and neglected in Scotland from 1999 to 2004 (as of 31 March 2004).

CHILDREN WHO HAVE A DISABILITY

Research suggests that children who have some form of disability are less likely to be placed on a Child Protection Register than non-disabled children (Cooke 1999; Cooke and Standen 2002). Many workers in child protection feel they have insufficient training in relation to disability and local authorities do not have well-articulated guidance in this area (Scottish Executive 2002d). It has also to be noted that statistical analyses do not account for a child's disability status in relation to official figures unless they are a looked after child.

A child with a disability is first and foremost a child. Having any form of disability means that you are more vulnerable than a child who does not have a disability. Children with a disability may be at greater risk of abuse and neglect for a number of reasons. They may be unable to communicate their needs effectively as a result of their disability and are likely to be heavily dependent upon their parents/carers or others for many of their basic requirements, including feeding and changing. These practical realities create situations which are potentially abusive and the child, because of the limitations imposed upon

Continued

them by their disability, may have no means of either protecting themselves or of alerting others to their plight.

At the wider organisational and societal level, existing procedures governing child protection need to incorporate an increased awareness of the particular issues facing children with a disability. Current systems and structures need to be flexible and appropriately attuned to these issues and practitioners require specialist training to be able to respond appropriately and effectively (Kennedy 1995; Scottish Executive 2002d) within a multi-agency context (Abbott et al. 2005) (see also Article 23 UNCRC).

The impact and consequences of child abuse and neglect

Being the victim of child abuse and neglect is a unique experience. It affects everyone differently. How people react and respond to their experiences will depend on a range of factors including their own personalities and psychology, the nature of the abuse, the context of their experiences and the support or otherwise they have around them. What follows is a list of some of the things that can happen following an experience of abuse and neglect. This list cannot do justice to the realities of being the victim of abuse and neglect, and I do not wish to reduce these experiences to words on a page. Rather, I want to illustrate the types of things people can experience following abuse and neglect in the context of having at the forefront of your mind the real pain and distress such incidents can cause; sometimes for the rest of a person's life. Child abuse and neglect are not a one-off event; it is a life-altering experience, and one which can change the lives not only of the victims, but of their families and friends. The consequences of any form of abuse can be seen as being immediate and longer-term. In relation to the former, we would include here physical and psychological manifestations occurring whilst the abuse is being perpetrated, whilst longer-term sequelae would be those manifestations which arise once the abuse has stopped but which nonetheless have an impact upon the individual in a number of ways.

Physical abuse and physical neglect

The most obvious consequence of physical abuse is the risk of injury or death. In many instances, injuries found in particular places are often indicative of child abuse. Remember that all children get cuts and bruises; some even get broken bones and worse. These things are part of life and happen at times. However, for a child who is being physically abused it is often the nature (non-accidental), type, location, severity and frequency of the injuries which can be telling. As a social worker, you need to be able to spot these signs; that does not mean you need to be able to give a definitive diagnosis: that is the job of medical staff. The practitioner (and that could be a professional from any agency) needs to be able to identify those signs and symptoms which appear to be suggestive of something wrong. This requires an appreciation of the context within which you may note an injury and the capacity to be able to raise this with the parent, either at the time or very soon thereafter if you feel that to do so too early might put the child at an even greater risk before you alert colleagues to the situation. These situations demand critical thinking skills from you, the practitioner. You have to assess risk (see below) and make a judgement about what to do (or not to do) next in highly pressured circumstances.

Characteristically, non-accidental injuries may present in particular ways. For example, there may be specific patterns of bruising; 'finger-tip' bruising is common where a child has been grabbed very harshly. This can be seen around the mouth and cheek area when a child is being force-fed, for example. Other mouth injuries can be a tear to the frenulum (under the tongue), again, often associated with forced feeding. These types of injuries would not necessarily just be associated with children who are very young. Children who have some form of disability and require assistance with feeding may also suffer these types of injury.

Other characteristic features would be bruising in the shape of an implement; bruising and swelling to the ears and burns, particularly to areas like the hands; or those of a particular shape such as those associated with cigarettes. Internal injuries may manifest via swellings or head injuries, via drowsiness, vomiting and other symptoms. These might be associated with 'shaken baby syndrome' (Wheeler 2003). This is where a child suffers head injuries and/or damage to the eyes as a result of being violently shaken.

In all of these presentations the issue is whether any injury has a reasonable explanation and whether the parent or carer has acted as any reasonable person ought to act in those situations to deal with it. Even if a child falls accidentally and suffers a nasty cut, the parent should respond. If not, there might be an issue of the parent physically neglecting the child and it could be argued that their failure to respond appropriately or their failure to afford the child reasonable protection from foreseeable danger is, in and of itself, abusive. The issue of reasonableness concerning explanations is an issue which has a limited frame of reference. If a child is repeatedly injured even though the explanation appears to fit the facts, questions might need to be asked about the parents' protective capacities. It is also likely that the whole issue of reasonable chastisement might need to be considered.

Sexual abuse

Sexual abuse is a phenomenon which is possibly the most difficult to work with for a variety of reasons. There are of course many taboos operating with regards to sex and sexuality in Western cultures and the use of children for the sexual gratification of adults is just such a taboo, legitimised by the force of law. The particular cultural context of this form of abuse makes it that much more difficult to identify, respond to and deal with. Furthermore, the contextual elements (taboo) reinforce the need for secrecy where such abuse is being perpetrated, thus generating added dimensions of complexity.

Common indicators of child sexual abuse include spontaneous disclosures by the child relating to sexual activity. It is important for you to remember that here again context is important. Depending upon the age of the child, there are some forms of knowledge and activity that would be highly suggestive that all is not well. For example, a 6-year-old who uses highly sexualised language and behaviours should raise concerns. These things in and of themselves would not mean that the child is or has been sexually abused, but in context, should prompt further inquiry. Conversely, a 15-year-old displaying knowledge of sexual activity might be more normative, particularly in the 21st century. Having said that, however, this should not be brushed aside either and depending upon the broader family situation and knowledge of the child, might or might not warrant further inquiry.

If there are physical signs of sexual abuse, these might appear as bruising to the genital area, bleeding or some form of infection. Here again, context specificity is important. Young children do not contract sexually transmitted diseases unless there is some form of sexual activity.

Sexual abuse does not just appertain to sexual contact. If children are being exposed to pornography or involved in any form of activity which has a sexual component or is sexualised, then concerns should be raised. It is inappropriate for children to be engaged in any form of activity which has a sexual content.

Importantly, there are a number of other indicators of child sexual abuse which may manifest in a number of ways, often as a result of emotional and/or psychological pressures and concerns. A child or young person may attempt to harm themselves or display behavioural changes which are not readily accounted for. It is in situations like these that good interpersonal skills are required by the practitioner to enable them to engage with the young person and assess the situation effectively.

There are a range of other consequences which relate to the distortion of relationships and family/other dynamics as a result of child sexual abuse. Whilst there may well be a range of physical signs that might indicate the presence of sexual abuse, it is often the behavioural manifestations that are the first indicator, and the interpretation of these can be a challenging task. These manifestations may be the result of changes to the family dynamics. If a child is being abused by someone from within the family (*intra-familial abuse*) then the perpetrator may well have told the child to keep the activity a secret. Very often the child will be told that if they speak out, the family will break up and it will be their fault. This can create an atmosphere of deception, betrayal and mistrust which can be very difficult to cope with. Even for mature adults, living in environments like this can be very challenging; for a developmentally and cognitively immature child (relatively speaking), it can be extremely hazardous. Mental health difficulties are not uncommon in children who are or have been the victims of sexual abuse.

These types of situation can have deleterious consequences on a child's well-being in many different ways, and serve to illustrate the (potentially crippling) complexity of family dysfunction and dynamics in situations involving child abuse, but particularly child sexual abuse.

Emotional abuse and neglect

It is arguable that emotional abuse and neglect are the most common form of abuse and yet they are probably the most difficult to quantify (Brown and Lynch 1998; Cawson 2002; Sidebotham 2000; Tanner and Turney 2003; (Wolock and Horowitz 1984) and to define and operationalise (Dubovitz et al. 2005; Scourfield 2000; Stone 1998; Straus and Kantor 2005).

In definitional and operational terms it is useful to be able to distinguish emotional abuse from emotional neglect, although both tend to co-exist and in other forms of child abuse and neglect there will inevitably be some element of emotional abuse and/or neglect.

Where emotional abuse exists, this presupposes a degree of intentionality from the abuser, whereas emotional neglect suggests a lack of awareness or a lack of emotional availability on the part of the parent/carer (Garbarino et al. 1986; Iwaniec 1995; O'Hagan 1993). The particular causes of emotional abuse and neglect need to be taken into account when responding to situations like this although, irrespective of these, if unchecked, both have the capacity to cause significant harm to a child.

Much research has illuminated our thinking about the consequences of emotional abuse and neglect (Berry et al. 2003; Iwaniec 1997; Iwaniec and Herbert 1999; Stevenson 1998; Stone 1998; Turney and Tanner 2001; Wood-Schneider et al. 2005). Broadly speaking, children tend to display low levels of self-esteem, relationship problems with their peers, increased rates of depression, anxiety and self-harm. In and of themselves these are problematic enough but it is important to be alive to the consequences of these factors. The compound nature of these difficulties can often lead to further problems arising as a result of attempts to cope with feelings of worthlessness. For example, if a child feels bad about themselves and as a result finds it difficult to make friends, they may well become the subject of bullying. This may well prompt them to try and deal with this by either withdrawing or becoming aggressive because of their sense of frustration and injustice. Such responses may well lead to further rejection and scapegoating by the parents/carers, which serves to deepen the misery as well as creating the potential for difficulties at school (Kendall-Tackett and Eckenrode 1996).

Over the long term, the impact of emotional abuse and neglect is correlated with depression, anxiety and other mental health problems including post-traumatic stress disorder, eating disorders, substance dependence and misuse, self-harm and suicidal behaviours as well as affecting general health (Briere 1992; Corby 2000; Kendall-Tackett 2002; Richardson 2005).

Other forms of abuse

All forms of abuse have negative consequences at some level. Individuals suffering the same form and level of abuse within a family may respond in different ways; individual differences in genetic, physical and psychological make-up may account for this phenomenon of multi-finality. One child may appear to be relatively unaffected by the abuse whilst another may well be severely damaged in a number of ways. As our understanding of the effects of abuse and neglect increase there are new and increasing demands made upon our practice. How we perceive the actions of others, how we define what is and is not abusive and/or neglectful and how we respond to these situations, strategically, definitionally and practically, all mean that as practitioners we must constantly be alive to the relative nature of this phenomenon and amend our practice accordingly.

We must also bear in mind that there are a range of factors residing within individuals and family situations which can contribute to the likelihood of abuse and neglect. These include domestic violence (Mullender et al. 2002), substance misuse (Harbin and Murphy 2000; Scottish Executive 2003c) and parental mental illness (Göpfert et al. 2000; Stanley et al. 2003).

Conclusion

The operational definitions, procedures and explanations concerning child abuse and neglect all contribute to the attempts by state agencies to manage a distinctly social phenomenon; to categorise something in order that it can be managed (Ashenden 2004; Scourfield and Welsh 2003). Clearly, the protection of children is something which has to be managed well. There are, however, a number of themes and issues which you need to consider in relation to the whole area of child protection.

Firstly, within each of the categories of abuse referred to above, it is possible to raise a host of different questions like: what do we mean by 'essential needs' or what constitutes a 'failure' to do something? How do we measure this and to what extent do 'essential needs' need to be met to be acceptable?

Secondly, the notion of state agencies being responsible for protecting children presupposes a number of things: that all children can be protected; that we know what it is we are protecting children from; that we know when children need to be protected; and that we are clear about how to protect them. We are not clear about all of these things all of the time. This is borne out by the litany of misery of many children over many years and offers testimony to this (unpalatable) fact. Irrespective of how complex our child protection systems are, there will always be incidents where children are harmed. The definitions referred to above appear to offer distinct categorisations and clear criteria against which actions can be measured. Upon closer inspection, however, there are a number of questions to be asked, as we have seen. What is clear is that some children do need to be protected from child abuse and neglect by the state because no one else will do it. It's everyone's job to make sure they're alright. As such, child protection needs to be located within a continuum of service delivery and within the broad scope of community responsibilities. Developments within Scotland are focusing upon the role of everyone in relation to the protection and well-being of children, professionally and publicly.

C H A P T E R   S U M M A R Y

In this chapter we have looked at child protection and the way it is responded to in Scotland. We have considered some of the underpinning theories and models utilised to assist us in understanding this phenomenon as well as looking at some of the effects child abuse and neglect can have upon people, as well as thinking about some of the reasons why it might occur.

FURTHER READING

Howe, **D** (2005) *Child abuse and neglect: attachment, development and intervention.* Basingstoke: Palgrave Macmillan.

An authoritative text which considers the issues of abuse and neglect through the lens of attachment theory.

Corby, **B** (2000) *Child abuse: towards a knowledge base (2nd edition).* Maidenhead: Open University Press.

A good introduction to the whole area of child abuse and neglect.

Chapter 5

Children in public care: looked after and accommodated children and young people

ACHIEVING A SOCIAL WORK DEGREE

This chapter will help you to meet the following Scottish Standards in Social Work Education (SiSWE) (Scottish Executive 2003a: available at www.scotland.gov.uk/library5/social/ffsw.pdf).

Key Role 1: Prepare for, and work with, individuals, families, carers, groups and communities to assess their needs and circumstances.

1:1 Preparing for social work contact and involvement.

1:2 Working with individuals, families, carers, groups and communities so they can make informed decisions.

1:3 Assessing needs and options in order to recommend a course of action.

Key Role 2: Plan, carry out, review and evaluate social work practice with individuals, families, carers, groups, communities and other professionals.

2:1 Identifying and responding to crisis situations.

2:2 Working with individuals, families, carers, groups and communities to achieve change, promote dignity, realise potential and improve life opportunities.

2:3 Producing, implementing and evaluating plans with individuals, families, carers, groups, communities and colleagues.

2:4 Developing networks to meet assessed needs and planned outcomes.

2:5 Working with groups to promote choice and independent living.

Key Role 4: Demonstrate professional competence in social work practice.

4:1 Evaluating and using up-to-date knowledge of, and research into, social work practice.

4:2 Working within agreed standards of social work practice.

4:3 Understanding and managing complex ethical issues, dilemmas and conflicts.

4:4 Promoting best social work practice, adapting positively to change.

Key Role 5: Manage and be accountable, with supervision and support, for their own social work practice within their organisation.

5:3 Contributing to the management of resources and services.

5:4 Managing, presenting and sharing records and reports.

5:5 Preparing for, and taking part in, decision-making forums.

5:6 Working effectively with professionals within integrated, multi-disciplinary and other service settings.

Introduction

This chapter will focus upon those children and young people who are looked after by the local authority. Within this notion of being looked after there is a distinction to be drawn between those children who are looked after *at home* with their own families and those who are looked after away from home and who are therefore accommodated by the local authority. This distinction is an important one and we shall look at both of these aspects, with a particular focus upon those children and young people who are looked after *away from home* and are therefore *accommodated*. In these situations children and young people may live with other families, often referred to as foster families, or they may live in a group setting in a residential unit or a 'children's home', as they were often called.

Legal and policy context

In relation to children and young people who are looked after and/or accommodated, the legal and policy context is quite complicated. However, what is of fundamental importance, particularly from the perspective of children and young people, is the issue of relationships. No amount of law or policy can legislate for positive relationships; these are predicated upon values, skills, knowledge, attitudes and the use of self (England 1986).

The main piece of legislation underpinning your practice in relation to looked after and accommodated children and young people is the Children (S) Act 1995, and section 17(6) defines what being looked after means:

> *Any reference in this Chapter of this Part to a child who is 'looked after' by a local authority, is to a child –*
>
> a) *for whom they are providing accommodation under section 25 of this Act;*
>
> b) *who is subject to a supervision requirement and in respect of whom they are the relevant local authority;*
>
> c) *who is subject to an order made, or authorisation or warrant granted, by virtue of Chapter 2, 3 or 4 of this Part of this Act, being an order, authorisation or warrant in accordance with which they have responsibilities as respects the child; or*
>
> d) *who is subject to an order in accordance with which, by virtue of regulations made under section 33(1) of this Act, they have such responsibilities.*

(Reproduced under the terms of Crown Copyright Policy Guidance issued by HMSO).

Section 25(8) of the 1995 Act defines what is meant by the term accommodation: 'In this Part of this Act, accommodation means, except where the context otherwise requires, accommodation provided for a continuous period of more than twenty-four hours', and section 26 defines the manner or form that accommodation may take, which includes placing the child or young person with a family, a relative or any other suitable person or in a residential establishment. These and other arrangements are themselves governed by a number of regulations, including:

- The Children (S) Act 1995 Regulations and Guidance: Volume 2 – Children Looked After by Local Authorities

- The Arrangements to Look After Children (S) Regulations 1996

- The Fostering of Children (S) Regulations 1996

- The Residential Establishments – Child Care (S) Regulations 1996

- The Secure Accommodation (S) Regulations 1996

- The Children's Hearings (S) Rules 1996

- Children's Hearings (Transmission of Information etc.) (S) Regulations 1996

- The Children (Reciprocal Enforcement of Prescribed Orders etc. (England and Wales and Northern Ireland)) (S) Regulations 1996

- Children's Hearings (Legal Representation) (S) Rules 2001/2002

- The Support and Assistance of Young People Leaving Care (S) Regulations 2003.

Section 73 of the Regulation of Care (S) Act 2001 has made amendments to section 29 of the Children (S) Act 1995 in order to enhance the provision of services to those children and young people who are ceasing to be looked after or accommodated (pathway planning) and section 6 of the Children (Leaving Care) Act 2000 (UK) extends to Scotland and refers to issues around financial provision.

The legal and policy context is derived in large measure from the need to regulate the public care of vulnerable children in order to ensure a consistency of approach and a guarantee of protection. However, as history has repeatedly informed us, no amount of law and policy can guarantee either of these things without reference to safe, ethical and theoretically informed practice underpinned by positive relationships and a respect for persons. Those children and young people who are looked after and/or accommodated are amongst the most vulnerable individuals in society and the state has both a legal duty (section 17 of the 1995 Act) and a moral responsibility to care for and protect them. Thus, we arrive at the interface of policy and practice.

Why do some children and young people have to be looked after?

In Chapter 2 we saw how the children's hearing system operated and why some children may be referred to it. In Chapter 3 we looked at how support may be offered to children, young people and their families and how this might involve the use of formal measures (supervision requirements). Thus, if a child or young person is made subject to a supervision requirement they become looked after by the local authority even though they may continue to live at home with their own family. The term is perhaps best considered differently from the normal understanding of the phrase; in this context the local authority are legally obliged to 'look after' the child's interests, even though the family may still be looking after them physically. Section 17 of the 1995 Act defines what the duties of the local authority are in this regard:

- to safeguard and promote the child's welfare;

- to make use of all available services;

- to ensure that personal relations between the child and those people who are significant in his or her life are promoted and maintained so long as this is consistent with the child's welfare;

- to provide the child with appropriate advice and assistance relevant to time and place and personal circumstances;

- to involve the child and other relevant people in decisions affecting them, taking account of their wishes (which is distinct from doing what the child wants to do);

- to take account of the child's religious, racial, cultural and linguistic background and heritage.

There are many reasons why a child or young person may become looked after or accommodated. In some circumstances the child and their family may feel that the best way to progress a difficult situation is for the child to spend some time away from home. This would be part of the overall care plan for the child and here the terms of section 25 of the 1995 Act would apply. Section 25 allows for the local authority to accommodate children and young people in the absence of legal orders made by the children's hearing or the courts in circumstances where:

- no one has parental responsibility for him or her (s.25(1)a));

- he or she is lost or abandoned (s.25(1)b));

- the person who has been caring for him or her is prevented from doing so for whatever reason (s.25(1)c)).

The use of section 25 is entirely consistent with the no-order principle and that of proportionality where such a course of action is felt to be appropriate and likely to work, i.e. to fulfil the stated aim(s).

CASE STUDY

Nathan is 11 years old. He lives at home with his mum, Helen. The social work department have been involved with the family for several months because of concerns first voiced by the school, who were worried about Nathan's care. It had been noticed that he was poorly dressed, dirty and unkempt and often appeared hungry. When in class, he would sometimes drop off to sleep and could not concentrate. An assessment by the social work department discovered that Helen found it difficult to motivate herself in the mornings and often slept in; Nathan had to get himself ready for school, which he found difficult to do. Mum had few routines in place and the home appeared chaotic, with visitors calling in at all times of the day and night. Attempts were made by the social work department to provide practical support to Helen but they had little effect although it was clear that she was trying. Over a period of time, despite the support, the situation continued to deteriorate. Agreement was reached that Nathan be accommodated under the terms of section 25 (1)c) of the Children (S) Act 1995 for a period to ensure that his needs were consistently met whilst work was undertaken with Helen to address the underlying difficulties.

Comment

In this situation, a point had been reached where despite the provision of home-based support, little improvement had been made. Helen had been cooperative to an extent but she just found it very difficult to get things together. Nathan was still being neglected and he needed to experience a period of consistent care which would improve his well-being. During his time in the care of the local authority Nathan had regular contact with his mum and after a period of several weeks, he returned home. Thereafter, the situation continued to improve with both Helen and Nathan receiving supports on a weekly basis.

In more serious circumstances a child's legal removal from home may be the only way to deal with a situation even where the child and their family disagree with this as a course of action. For example, a child may have been the victim of some form of abuse and neglect (see Chapter 4) and the home environment is such that the necessary safeguards to prevent this happening again are not available, because the parents are either unwilling or unable to provide such assurances. It may also be that the child themselves requires to be kept safe because of their own behaviour towards themselves and/or others. In these situations a children's hearing could make a supervision order with a specific condition attached to it stating that the child should live in a named place such as a residential school or a special secure unit. Such measures are only taken as a last resort or in those circumstances where the risks to the child or other people are very serious indeed. Where this does happen the child is a *looked after* child (by virtue of the imposition of a supervision requirement) who is *accommodated* by the local authority (by virtue of them being made to live in a place provided by the local authority). However, a child or young person can also become accommodated in an emergency by virtue of the terms of a Child Protection Order. In these situations the plan would always be to reunite the family as soon as possible so the period of accommodation would be deemed to be temporary until the protection issues can be resolved. This may not always work out though, and some children and young people may remain accommodated for some time.

CASE STUDY

Anna is 12 years old and lives with her parents and younger brother John, who is 9. She has been the victim of sexual abuse by a family friend who used to baby-sit on a regular basis. Following investigations by the social work department and the police, Anna disclosed what had happened in graphic detail. Subsequently, Anna has become very withdrawn, refusing to speak to people. Both her parents are of the opinion that she will just 'come round' in time. However, following a thorough assessment of the situation, the social worker is of the opinion that some specific work must be done to help Anna come to terms with what has happened. Her parents are at a loss. The social work department have referred Anna to the authority Reporter and a children's hearing has been convened. The social work department recommend to the hearing that Anna be made subject to a supervision requirement under the terms of section 70(1) of the Children (S) Act 1995 in order that they can work with Anna and her family whilst she remains at home.

> **CASE STUDY**
>
> *Alan is 14 years old. Over the past few months his behaviour has been giving everyone grave cause for concern. He is associating with a group of older males and refuses to return home. He has assaulted several young people who live locally and has also assaulted his mother on at least three occasions. He is drinking and using volatile substances. All attempts to engage with him have resulted in confrontations involving verbal abuse and threats of physical violence towards his social worker and the police, who have been called many times. Last week, Alan refused to attend the children's hearing. A warrant was issued for him to be detained in a place of safety in order that his attendance at a future hearing could be guaranteed. Once there, Alan refused point blank to engage with anyone. As a result of the situation and the concerns in evidence concerning his own well-being and that of others, Alan's supervision requirement was varied and he was detained, against his wishes, in a secure unit.*

Comment

These situations reflect different approaches involving the use of supervision requirements. In the first, Anna has suffered from abuse which has clearly traumatised her. It appears that her parents are concerned about her, but given the gravity of what has happened, perhaps feel overwhelmed and are unsure about what to do. The social worker feels that Anna needs a lot of support to get through this, as do the family, but believes that in order for the support to be as effective as possible, a supervision requirement would be useful and proportionate. The case has been referred to the authority Reporter as section 52(2)d) applies. The recommendation to the hearing is that a supervision requirement should be considered so that focused work can be undertaken with Anna and the family as part of a care plan which details what needs to happen, when, where, how and for how long, drawing upon and utilising a range of specialist resources. The regulations governing care plans are to be found in the Arrangements to Look After Children (S) Regulations 1996, especially regulation 6 and schedule 2.

In respect of Alan, his behaviour is becoming extreme. Despite a children's hearing having been arranged (ss.52(2) a), b), h), i), j) and k), all appear to apply) he refused to attend. He appears to be unwilling to work with anyone and the possibility of him remaining at home with his family appears remote, particularly since he absents himself from there regularly and has assaulted his mum. The chances of any workable solution to the situation being implemented whilst he is at home appear unlikely. He is putting himself (and others) at considerable risk. The social worker and the family feel that they have gone as far as they can go, having exhausted all attempts to work with Alan. The hearing has to consider whether removing Alan from his home is proportionate to what needs to happen in order to ensure his safety and well-being and, in this situation, the safety and well-being of others. Here, section 16(5) of the 1995 Act is relevant because this provision allows the hearing to make a decision which appears to run counter to the paramountcy principle of section 16(1) of the 1995 Act; in this case, that placing Alan in a secure unit against his own wishes would not appear to be in his best interests. However, in conjunction with the provisions available under section 70(9) and (10) of the 1995 Act, this is what the hearing decides to do. This is an extreme situation but one which does arise and does need to be addressed. The hearing could also utilise the measures which now exist under the terms of the Anti-Social Behaviour etc. (S) Act 2004 (see below).

Children and young people who are in public care

This section looks at those children and young people who are looked after away from home by the local authority, either because they are subject to a supervision requirement or some other emergency) order or because the terms of section 25 of the 1995 Act apply. Whenever a child or young person becomes looked after, the terms of section 17 of the 1995 Act automatically and always apply in relation to the local authority's duties towards them.

RESEARCH SUMMARY

Table 5.1 *The number of children looked after by accommodation type (as at 31 March each year)*

Year	At home (supervision requirements)	Foster care/ adopters	Friends/relatives	Residential care	Total
2000	5270	3181	1274	1585	11309
2001	4842	3280	1195	1582	10897
2002	4909	3328	1409	1595	11241
2003	4851	3468	1518	1550	11388
2004	4982	3608	1518	1567	11675

(*Source*: Scottish Executive: adapted from Table 1.3. Available at www.scotland.gov.uk/Resource/Doc/77843/ 0018789.pdf

---

Whilst there are clear guidelines on when a child or young person may need to be accommodated, we must also consider this in experiential terms: what does it mean to the child or young person concerned? In order to be able to provide an effective service you must not only be aware of the procedural elements governing such situations, but you must also be aware of the 'people' elements – those aspects which relate to thoughts, feelings and experiences. In this section we shall look at both of these aspects, the procedural and the personal, and integrate these into a coherent practice framework which can be used in relation to your practice in situations where children and young people need to be accommodated.

The procedural elements

There are a number of legal and regulatory matters to be taken into account in relation to the accommodation of children and young people. These are designed to assist in the implementation of a coherent and consistent approach. Central to this is the child's care plan. A care plan is a document drawn up in conjunction with the child or young person, their parents or carers and those who are to provide a service to them. This might include the social worker, foster carers or staff from a residential unit, the school, an educational or clinical psychologist or anyone else who it is felt has something to offer. Regulation 3 of the Arrangements to Look After Children (S) Regulations 1996 imposes a duty upon the local authority to make a care plan in respect of any child they look after or accommodate. This duty also applies to those children and young people who are subject to a supervision requirement at home, although here we shall focus upon its use within the context of children and young people who are accommodated. The elements of a care plan are specified in schedule 2 of the Regulations and include:

- personal and family details;

- details relating to nationality, race, religion and language;

- a physical description of the child;

- details concerning the legal situation of the child, past and present;

- details relating to past and present involvement with professionals or other service providers;

- details relating to the child's family and contact details;

- the child's health history;

- the child's educational history and current arrangements for education;

- details relating to the child's personality and social development;

- details relating to the child's interests.

All of this may appear to be somewhat formal and rather impersonal. These and other regulations map out the broad areas which it is felt are necessary to include in relation to basic information concerning a child or young person. Details are required in order that the people who will be caring for the child know something of them and their circumstances. This is the beginning of the process of getting to know the child and being in a position to respond appropriately to their needs as these become more apparent. This is the 'what'. How that information is obtained, recorded and subsequently utilised for the benefit of the child or young person represents the effective interface between the procedural and the personal aspects of such situations. In an attempt to make the obtaining of information more user-friendly and child-focused, the Department of Health developed a range of materials to be used with looked after and accommodated children entitled *Good parenting: good outcomes*, based upon one of the three dimensions of the Framework for Assessment of Children in Need and their Families (Department of Health 2000). Based upon this, the Integrated Assessment Framework (IAF) is now being developed in Scotland (Scottish Executive 2005d) and a range of guidance and other documentation is being made available which will complement and may ultimately replace the current materials (see Chapter 3).

The difficulties which can arise when information is either not shared or acted upon were evident in the case of the children living in the Western Isles whose situation was the subject of a recent Social Work Inspection Agency report (SWIA 2005) and the proposals currently being discussed are an attempt to minimise this happening again.

These materials (and others) attempt to offer a framework within which a consistent approach can be taken to recording important information about children and young people who are looked after and those who are accommodated. The means by which this is achieved has more to do with the 'how'; different professionals will approach the task differently depending upon their own particular practice base, underpinned by their experiences, knowledge, values and, importantly, skills in relation to engaging and interacting with children, young people and their families. The availability of various tools to assist practitioners in the collection and collation of valuable information is in itself no guarantee of the quality of this information or its value in terms of the use to which it might be put. This is about you and your people skills (Thompson 2002).

Any child or young person who is accommodated is a child whose situation is such as to have warranted concern. It should therefore come as no surprise to learn that a necessary part of the care plan is a comprehensive assessment used to underpin interventions in the child's life designed to promote their well-being. Having said that, it is important to pause for a moment and reflect upon this; any child who is experiencing difficulties in their life only really wants things to be sorted out. They do not want to be 'prodded and poked' during the assessment processes and made to feel worse than they might already feel in the wake of all the trauma and disruption they are likely to have experienced by talking about their lives and their experiences. It is recognised that this will happen and the majority of children and young people accept this. It is not a case therefore of whether it will happen, but when and how and it is these distinctions that can make the difference between the development of positive and productive relationships between professionals and children and young people, and those which serve only to depersonalise the child even more and cause greater damage. Empathy, sensitivity and knowing when and how to ask questions is a critical component of positive practice in terms of any assessment.

Foster care

As we have seen, there are situations and circumstances in a child's life which mean that they are unable to live at home with their own families. As a result the state, in the form of local authorities, has a legal (and moral) obligation to provide for them. Placing a child or young person with another family is referred to as foster care.

The practice of foster care recognises that the majority of children and young people in the UK normally live within family settings so this arrangement attempts to replicate that practice by recognising that such arrangements can and do provide continuity, stability, care, protection and a sense of love and belongingness. Given that those children and young people who require substitute care are those who have experienced varying degrees of trauma and dislocation, the need for good-quality care is vital (Holland et al. 2005). It is also important to remember that families differ in many ways in terms of structure and function, dependent upon cultural beliefs and practices. Any foster placement for a child should be one which is as close to their own family arrangement as possible and so resources and plans need to take account of difference and diversity.

Michael is 7 years old. He has been accommodated following a children's hearing because of major concerns for his well-being as a result of poor parenting, parental substance misuse and a continuing decline in conditions at home. His parents have not cooperated with social work and other agencies. Michael is placed with a foster family who live on the other side of town and have three children of their own, a boy aged 10 and two girls aged 14 and 17 years.

Sarah is 12 and Dominic is 14. Both were removed from the care of their parents under an emergency Child Protection Order as a result of a serious incident of assault upon Dominic by his adoptive father. Both parents have blamed the children for causing problems in their marriage and accused Dominic of stealing from them. Sarah witnessed the events.

Jonathan is 9 days old. He has been abandoned by his parents and left at the local hospital.

Comment

In each of these situations all the children require to have their basic needs attended to. These of course will be slightly different as a result of their respective ages, but each requires safety, shelter, food and clothing. Michael's situation is one where it was anticipated that a foster placement might be required, so a family was identified prior to the hearing in the event that the panel members accepted the social work department's recommendations. Michael had been made aware that he might be staying with another family and had been given details about this in a manner consistent with his age and level of understanding. The foster family had been given information concerning Michael's situation and were able to make some preparations for his arrival. For example, they had prepared his room and were waiting for him to arrive. They were also aware of where he went to school and other basic information which assisted them in making Michael feel a little more comfortable. Prior to the hearing, Michael had asked his social worker whether he would still be going to the same school and whether he would be allowed to take some personal effects with him. This was discussed with Michael and he was allowed to pack a big bag with his clothes and toys in it. When he arrived at his foster home, the family took an interest in his arrival and helped him to unpack his things. He remained at the same school so he did not have to worry about making new friends and getting to know new teachers. Michael also asked about the other children in the house.

Sarah and Dominic had been involved in a very traumatic incident and both ended up being removed suddenly from their homes. There had been no opportunity for any forward planning and both Sarah and Dominic were only told where they would be staying whilst they were being driven to the foster placement, which was some 20 miles away. They arrived late in the evening with very few personal possessions beyond what they could take as they left the house. This meant that they left behind school things and those personal items we all treasure, like favourite photos, books and 'stuff'. When they arrived, they were tired and traumatised. The foster family made them feel welcome and made them both as comfortable as possible. Both Sarah and Dominic didn't know what was to happen next. They were unsure whether they would be going back home, whether they would be going back to their school, and they had lots of feelings they did not know what to do with. The social worker and the foster carers spoke with them and gave as much information as they could but both children were very unsettled, displaying signs of loss and struggling to cope with the sudden and massive changes forced upon them.

Jonathan, after remaining in the hospital for a week, was placed with a foster family nearby under the terms of section 25 of the 1995 Act. He was a little unsettled whilst his routine was established. He was seen by the health visitor and appeared to be doing well. The local authority along with the police made efforts to find his parents.

All of the children and young people here have suffered trauma which has resulted in them having to stay with other families, for very different reasons. All of them have basic needs relating to their safety and protection and the older children also have a need to understand what has happened as well as what will happen (Jewett 1984). In the case of Michael, there was some opportunity to address these needs; with respect to Sarah and Dominic this was not possible as their need for safety was overwhelming and no planning was possible.

As you can see from the above case studies, the experience of being accommodated brings with it its own traumas in addition to those which led to the situation in the first place. Once a child or young person is in placement with a family it is important to ensure that good relationships are established and maintained with the child, their family and those other significant people in their lives, including friends and schools. In some situations, contact by the child with their family may not be safe or it may only be able to take place under certain conditions, for example, if supervised by a social worker (Macaskill 2002). It may also be the case that the child has been placed some distance from their home, resulting in a need for them to change schools. Ideally, these situations should not occur because having to change school is in itself a major transition and not one entered into lightly; having to move schools in the wake of major trauma can often cause further difficulties. The realities are, however, that these things do happen and it is up to the professionals involved and the foster carers to be appreciative of these additional burdens and to help the child manage this situation as best they can.

RESEARCH SUMMARY

Becoming a foster carer

In order to become a foster carer, individuals and their families must be approved by the local authority within which they reside. There are a number of regulations and procedures governing this process which are designed to ensure that foster carers are not only safe and suitable to care for very vulnerable children and young people, but also that they are resourceful and resilient enough to cope with the demands that this type of work entails. The Fostering of Children (S) Regulations 1996 specify the various requirements placed upon local authorities to recruit, assess, approve and support foster carers.

Continued

> *The Regulations also refer to the requirements for placing a child or young person in foster care on both a planned basis and in emergency situations.*
>
> *There are also the National Care Standards for Foster Care and Family Placement Services (Scottish Executive 2005f) which outline the kind of services people can expect to receive, as well as guidance and information from the Fostering Network (www.thefostering.net).*

Moving into foster care

Moving into a new family situation can be difficult. New families bring with them new faces, new places, new routines, new and different expectations and new rules. Some children may well have come from situations where there were no rules in their families; chaos may have reigned supreme so the (relatively) new appearance of rules may be something of a shock and may cause a reaction. A previous absence of routine, structure, predictability, care, concern and graded independence suddenly replaced by an environment which has this in abundance requires adaptation (Cairns 2002; Doyle 1997; Richardson and Bacon 2001). Behaviour may become challenging as the child seeks ways of making sense of their changed situation. Children and young people who have been abused and neglected often find it difficult to trust people; this may also reflect other difficulties associated with attachment problems (Crittenden 1992; Golding 2003; Howe 2005) and may reflect the child or young person's need to test out the boundaries in terms of what is acceptable or not in relation to how safe and secure their position is. Foster carers are usually able to recognise these things for what they are but that does not necessarily make it any easier to deal with. Recognising distress is one thing; containing and dealing with it can be another and can sometimes make placements difficult to sustain (Ironside 2004).

Bad behaviour, swearing, stealing, aggression, self-harm and running away may be signs that the child is finding it difficult to cope, and if these situations become unmanageable the child or young person may need to be moved somewhere else, thus reinforcing their perception that they are unlovable or otherwise 'bad' because they have been rejected again. It is a difficult balance to achieve between trying to offer the child or young person a stable, caring and supportive home whilst recognising that the needs of the foster family, as a family in their own right, need to be supported (Jackson and Thomas 1999).

Kinship care

In some circumstances, member(s) of the child's extended family may be able to offer a place for the child in their home. If this is felt to be appropriate, then the regulations allow for this to happen providing that the relatives are approved in a similar way to that required in relation to non-family members, although the current requirements are not as stringent. This latter point has recently been the subject of much debate in both Scotland and other parts of the UK. The case of Victoria Climbié in England who was severely abused and neglected by her aunt and her boyfriend until her tragic death brought this issue to the headlines. Victoria's aunt was looking after her and because of the family tie, the local authority in whose area Victoria resided did not pursue any assessment or approval process in relation to their suitability as carers. Similar issues were recently highlighted in Scotland (SWIA 2005). The recommendations from these reports highlight the need for more rigour in terms of the assessment of relatives as carers with less weight being given to implicit assumptions by professionals that as these people are 'family' then things are likely to be OK. This so-called 'rule of optimism' on the part of professionals has been a cause for concern over a number of years (Blom-Cooper 1985) and represents one of the dilemmas inherent in the task of providing effective services for highly vulnerable children in a world where resources can be scarce and the need to provide the child or young person with as much security as possible can appear to be resolved by the offer of a placement from a family member.

The kinship bond may well be an issue to consider in a positive light (Inglehart 1994; Ryburn 1998), but clearly this should not obscure the need for an objective view of the motives, capacities and intent of even the most apparently devoted relative.

The care of children and young people in the foster care situation is a demanding and challenging task. Many children respond favourably to their experiences of foster care (Schofield 2001) and indeed some see it as the only experience they have had where safety, security, consistency, attention and love and affection were commonplace.

Residential care

Some children and young people who are accommodated may be cared for in a residential unit in a group care setting. This arrangement has often been seen as something of a 'Cinderella service' in comparison to fostering services. According to Brown et al. (1998), this may be because there are difficulties in 'establishing a unified theory of residential care' because 'there is no one task to be achieved and no single method of producing good results' (p2). Some feel that residential child care is in many ways seen as a last resort; somewhere to turn to if there are no other options available, whereas others argue that it should be seen as a positive choice, offering a valuable service to those who require that which it can offer.

What is residential care?

According to Kendrick and Fraser (1992), it is difficult to determine with any degree of accuracy what residential child care is. They base this view on the fact that the term appears to encompass a wide range of types of provision so that specificity is difficult. They argue that '(I)t is important to focus more directly on specific types of residential provision and examine their strengths and weaknesses' (p103). However, it is perhaps useful here to provide a general overview of what residential child care looks like before considering specific types of it which are designed to respond to particular types of need.

A residential childcare unit is a place specifically designed and/or operated for the sole purpose of looking after children and young people who cannot live at home. It differs from foster care in that it will usually have a staff team on site who support the residents, and will be occupied by a number of young people at any one time, most of whom are unrelated. All residential settings are regularly inspected and are required to meet the standards set down in the National Care Standards: Care Homes for Children and Young People (Scottish Executive 2005g) and comply with the legislative requirements arising from the Regulation of Care (S) Act 2001. These standards, along with the National Care Standards: School Care

Accommodation Services (Scottish Executive 2005h), form the basic tools for the regulatory activities of the Scottish Commission for the Regulation of Care (the Care Commission) in relation to the inspection of residential settings. These standards have been prepared as a means by which services can audit themselves. They have been written from the perspective of the children and young people who use these services, which is a progressive step forward in relation to service user involvement in service audit (Maclean 2002).

Types of residential provision

The provision of residential childcare has something of a chequered history (Abrams 1998) and there have been a number of major scandals and inquiries into this type of provision which have left many professionals and others of the view that such service provision is not the first choice when a child or young person needs to be accommodated (see Corby et al. 2001; Scottish Office 1992, 1997b). There are many perceptions that residential childcare is only suitable for those who are aggressive or difficult or who have special needs. The reality is different: the choice of residential accommodation should be a positive choice and one which reflects the best available service to meet the needs of a child or young person at any given time in any given circumstance. All Integrated Children's Services Plans produced by local authorities must promote residential childcare as a positive option to be considered in appropriate circumstances.

There will always be some individuals who find the relative intimacy of a family-type setting as in foster care more challenging or intimidating. This may well reflect their earlier experiences of family-based care prior to being accommodated or the fact that they have had several disrupted family placements and therefore find that type of setting difficult to manage. These realities mean that there can be no hard and fast rules concerning which provision should be used for whom and when. These decisions should arise from the process of assessment. It is, however, important to recognise that the benefits of a family-based placement are likely to be more appropriate for younger children (under 12) who have far less experience than older children in relating to adults they do not know. The very nature of residential units means that there will be changing faces over the course of each day due to shift patterns and young(er) children require a stronger sense of continuity than could be guaranteed in these placements. Therefore, family placement is seen as the preferred choice for all children under the age of 12 (Scottish Office 1992).

CASE STUDY

David is 13 years old. He is currently in a foster placement (his third one in the last six months) which is showing signs of strain. Both David and his foster carers have recognised that there are difficulties between them relating to David's previous experiences of family care which have resulted in him being very confrontational and aggressive when he is challenged concerning the most routine matter. For example, when he is told to hurry up in the mornings to get ready for school or when in the evenings he is asked to turn his music down to an acceptable level, he will become verbally aggressive and threatening. David is resistant to all attempts to calm him and David invariably ends up breaking things and threatening the foster carers' children, who are several years younger than he. It has been agreed that a residential unit be made available for David.

CASE STUDY

Sally is 14 years old. She has experienced prolonged periods of emotional abuse and neglect within her family. Discussions have taken place with the family and Sally concerning a placement for her. She expressed the view that she would like to go to a residential unit because the thought of going into a strange family would be too much for her just now as she feels very guilty about what is happening in her life, even though she is not to blame.

Another variation is that of a residential school which provides accommodation; a boarding school-type arrangement. These units' main function would be seen as the provision of education but there is a significant commitment to the care aspect. Many young people in these schools may well return to their own homes or foster homes or other residential units at weekends or holidays and thereby receive what might be referred to as 'shared care', with the majority of it provided away from home.

For some young people there is secure accommodation. This is where care and education are provided on one site which is highly structured and secure, i.e. locked. This type of provision is highly regulated and only used where young people are deemed to be a significant danger to themselves and/or others. Its use in respect of such youngsters is through the children's hearing system or the courts and is regularly reviewed and only used as long as it is deemed to be necessary.

There are also a range of residential units and schools which are referred to as therapeutic communities. They offer care and education within one site but do so within a particular therapeutic milieu which offers treatment for particular issues (Hazler and Barwick 2001; Trieschman et al. 1969).

In many ways, irrespective of the type of residential provision made available, good-quality care is at the heart of this. As a result of a review of residential childcare in the 1990s (Scottish Office 1992), a number of principles were established which are now seen to underpin good practice in this area. You can read the 'Skinner principles' in the box below.

RESEARCH SUMMARY

The Skinner principles
Another kind of home: a review of residential child care (*Scottish Office 1992*) *led by Angus Skinner, referred to eight fundamental principles which should underpin residential childcare and provide a framework within which good practice can develop (p21):*

Individuality and development: *all those youngsters in residential care have the right to be treated as individuals 'who have their own unique relationships, experiences, strengths, needs and futures, irrespective of the needs of other residents'. One of the tasks of residential care is to prepare them for the future.*

Rights and responsibilities: *every child and young person, along with their parent's/carers 'should be given a clear statement of their rights and responsibilities'. There should also be confidential means by which and through which those in receipt of the service can complain. It is also important that all concerned are involved in decisions which affect the child's life.*

Continued

Good basic care: *all those children and young people in residential care of any sort should receive a high standard of personal care. This should include access to new and varied experiences which promotes their development and integration within the wider community.*

Education: *all children and young people should be 'actively encouraged' in all aspects of their education. This relates also to vocational training and employment opportunities.*

Health: *the health needs of those in residential care should be identified and met with encouragement to develop healthy lifestyles.*

Partnership with parents: *all children and young people in residential care should receive care which has the potential to maximise the involvement of their parents where this is in their interests.*

Child-centred collaboration: *all children and young people 'should be able to rely upon a high quality of inter-disciplinary teamwork amongst the adults providing for their care, education and health needs'.*

A feeling of safety: *children and young people in any form of residential provision should feel safe and secure.*

(Adapted from Scottish Office 1992, p21)

Comment

These principles were and still are seen as being important statements concerning the provision of residential childcare services. Since these were presented in 1992 there have been many developments (Scottish office 1997b) which have strengthened these and added to them, including children's rights officers, and the advent of the Commissioner for Children and Young People (S) Act 2003 has provided the legislative basis for the appointment of a Commissioner for Children and Young People who is independent of the Scottish Executive.

RESEARCH SUMMARY

The Scottish Commissioner for Children and Young People

The first Scottish Commissioner for Children and Young People was appointed in April 2004. The role of the Commissioner is to promote and safeguard the rights of children and young people in Scotland by:

- *generating awareness of the rights of children and young people;*
- *looking at the adequacy and effectiveness of law, policy and practice as this relates to the rights of children and young people;*
- *promoting best practice;*
- *commissioning and undertaking research.*

Appointments such as these reinforce the centrality of children's rights in terms of their relationship to practice.

Working in residential childcare

The range of residential provision is quite wide and aims to offer specialised services to children and young people geared towards their individual and, in some cases, highly complex needs (Kendrick 2002).

Working within residential care is a very demanding and sometimes challenging occupation. It requires great skill in terms of interpersonal relationships, communication and working with groups of people. The hours can be long and the demands great. There can also be a great sense of achievement and when a home is well run and the children and young people who reside there feel that this is working for them, the whole experience can be very positive. Quality care is what counts (Watson 2003).

Permanency

Whether a child or young person is cared for in a family-based placement or some form of residential provision will be determined by a range of factors. Some of these youngsters will be unable to return home and will be too young for there to be any thought of independent living at that time. For these children and young people permanent care outside of their family will have to be made available. How that is achieved is determined by the particular needs of the child or young person, the type of placement identified and the legal means used to underpin the placement.

The arrangements available to secure this permanency of care are underpinned by a range of legal measures, some of which are more supportive of permanency than others. Basically, the arrangements which are available all hinge upon the care arrangements for the child, and the younger the child, the more there is a need to consider options like adoption as opposed to long-term fostering arrangements. Other options which exist in relation to permanence fall into those which apply in respect of private individuals and those which refer to local authorities. Table 5.2 summarises all of the options currently available.

Table 5.2 *Current options in relation to permanency*

Individual application	Local authority application
s.11(2)b) Children (S) Act 1995 (Parental Responsibilities and Parental Rights)	s.86(1) Children (S) Act 1995 (Parental Responsibilities Order)
s.11(2)c) Children (S) Act 1995 (Residence Order)	s.18(5) Adoption (S) Act 1978 (Freeing for Adoption Order)
s.11(2)d) Children (S) Act 1995 (Contact Order)	s.70 Children (S) Act 1995 (Supervision Requirement)
s.11(2)h) Children (S) Act 1995 (Guardianship Order)	
s.30(9) Human Fertilisation and Embryology Act 1990 (Parental Order)	
s.12(3) Adoption (S) Act 1978 (Adoption Order)	

All of these options offer permanency to a greater or lesser extent. Those which are in the 'individual' column are orders applied for to the Sheriff Court by private individuals. The orders available under the terms of section 11 of the Children (S) Act 1995 include orders relating to the granting of parental responsibilities and rights to individuals, orders which state where and with whom a child will live (residence), orders which regulate who any child shall and/or shall not have any contact with (contact order) and orders appointing another as the child's legal guardian. These are the main orders under the terms of section 11 of the Children (S) Act 1995 which can facilitate a degree of permanency, often used in conjunction with each other in a variety of ways. The net effect of approaching permanency in this way is one which is rather fragmented and piecemeal, constantly open to legal challenge where the real parent's circumstances change. Thus, whilst these orders may confer parental status upon the substitute carers, they do not guarantee that the arrangement will be permanent.

The Parent Order referred to in relation to the Human Fertilisation and Embryology Act 1990 is one which confers the legal status of 'parent' upon an individual who had engaged in a surrogacy agreement. All legal responsibilities and rights held initially by the biological parent are extinguished and transferred to the legal parent(s). In many respects, this type of order is very similar to the effect of an adoption order.

Adoption is where the legal rights of the biological parent(s) in respect of a child are removed by a court order and vested in another. Currently, the Adoption (S) Act 1978 is the main source of adoption law in Scotland along with relevant sections of the Children (S) Act 1995 and the Adoption and Children Act 2002 (UK). Once this has been done by the court the biological parent(s) have no further claim(s) in respect of the child and the adoptive parent(s) become the child's new legal parent(s). Obviously, no court order is able to remove the biological connection between a parent and a child but in terms of legal responsibilities and rights (see ss.1 and 2, Children (S) Act 1995) an adoption order is final and cannot (ordinarily) be challenged. Any plan for adoption would relate to a child or young person being in a family-based placement.

BUT WHAT DOES 'PERMANENCY' REALLY MEAN?

The discussion in this section has made several references to the notion of permanency and said that this is achieved by recourse to legal measures. But is that the reality? Does permanency not depend upon enduring relationships, irrespective of the imposition of court orders? The short answer is 'yes'. When we refer to permanency this is often used as a kind of shorthand to indicate the type of measures put in place to ensure that the child or young person is in a placement with substitute carers which will not be open to challenge.

However, adoption is generally all or nothing. There have been developments over the past few years which have looked at how security and stability can be offered to children and young people who cannot live with their own families without necessarily going down this route. Adoption is not suitable for everyone in much the same way that long-term fostering is not suitable for everyone. Recently, adoption practice has sought to recognise that although a child or young person may need the security and stability

Continued ▷

105

> *offered by an adoption order, some children struggle with the notion that that is the end of their relationship with their biological parents, sometimes irrespective of how bad things might have been whilst they were cared for by them. Similarly, the practices where adoption records were unavailable to those people who had been adopted have now been modified to recognise that a person's need to know who their real parents were can become all-consuming. The need to have a clear sense of who you are and where you came from is recognised as being an important part of healthy identity formation and maintenance (Neil 2000) as well as a contributor to positive mental health. The quality of adoption services is regulated by the National Care Standards: Adoption Agencies (Scottish Executive 2005i).*

In relation to those options for permanency which can be facilitated by the actions of the local authority, the least secure is that of maintaining a child or young person on a supervision requirement with a named place of residence inserted into the order. These requirements are automatically reviewed after a year, and can be reviewed every three months if the child's parents or the child decide to ask for a review. And whilst there are mechanisms in place to discourage unnecessary reviews, the use of repeated supervision requirements is not seen to be good practice.

Another solution is the application by the local authority for a Parental Responsibilities Order. If granted, this means that the local authority is invested with some or all of the responsibilities and rights of the natural parents (with some exceptions) and is expected to act as any reasonable parent would in the fulfilment of those duties. This means that the local authority is the child or young persons' corporate parent and this arrangement may well be appropriate in some circumstances, particularly if a parent (or relevant person) cannot be found or:

> *has persistently failed, without reasonable cause, to fulfil one or other of the following parental responsibilities in relation to the child, that is to say the responsibility to safeguard and promote the child's health, development and welfare or, if the child is not living with him, the responsibility to maintain personal relations and direct contact with the child on a regular basis (s86(2)b)iii))*

or (that person)

> *has seriously ill-treated the child, whose reintegration into the same household as that person is, because of the serious ill-treatment or for other reasons, unlikely (s86(2)b)iv)).*

Such an order may also be made if all the relevant persons concerned agree to it. It is worth remembering that a supervision requirement does not remove any parental responsibilities or rights from the parent(s), although it may interfere with their capacity to implement these, whereas a section 86 order can, subject to these being specified by the Sheriff. Generally speaking, these orders are time-limited and often made in circumstances where adoption would not be appropriate.

In situations where it is felt that the making of an adoption order in respect of a child is the best course of action, an application for an adoption order under the terms of section

12(3) can be made. In any such application there are a number of conditions which must be met, one of which is that the consent of the natural parent(s) must be obtained before an application can proceed. If the parent(s) refuse to agree to this then in some circumstances the court can grant what is referred to as a Freeing Order, which allows the child to be adopted even in the face of parental opposition. In order for this to happen the court has to be satisfied that adoption is in the best interests of the child and that the parent(s) are withholding their consent unreasonably. What is deemed to be unreasonable is a complicated issue and one which the courts need to unravel. The court has to decide whether, in all the circumstances, the adoption plan is right for the child and that the parents' opposition is unreasonable given all the facts. If the court so decides, then an order under section 18(5) of the Adoption (S) Act 1978 is made freeing the child for adoption. This has the effect of removing all parental responsibilities and rights from the natural parent(s), vesting these in the local authority until such time as a full adoption order is granted upon application by suitable adopters.

RESEARCH SUMMARY

The Adoption Policy Review

The law on adoption is currently under review in Scotland. The Adoption Policy Review began in 2001 and is making recommendations concerning the law and practice relating to adoption and other means of obtaining permanency for those children and young people who cannot live at home with their parents. The aim of the group is to review current practice in the light of experience and in the context of changes within society more generally. The review has made a number of recommendations including the creation of a new legal order, a Permanence Order, which will replace the current Parental Responsibilities Order and be more flexible. Other recommendations relate to who can be considered as prospective adopters, including same-sex and unmarried couples. There are also a number of recommendations which relate to court procedures and the role of the children's hearing system in adoption cases.

In considering the long-term needs of a child or young person, planning is essential. During the time a child or young person is being looked after and accommodated, regular reviews are essential. These statutory reviews are governed by the terms of section 31 of the 1995 Act and form the basis of the planning process. The looked after children materials referred to above assist in this process. Any plan which has adoption as a consideration must conform to the guidance issued by the Scottish Executive (Scottish Office 1997c) and be compliant with the Adoption Agencies (S) Regulations 1996.

Moving on: throughcare and aftercare

In response to the experiences of young people and the findings of research over a number of years (Biehal et al. 1992, 1995; Dixon and Stein 2002; Millham et al. 1986; Strathdee and Johnson 1994), a more concerted effort has been made to respond to the particular issues surrounding 'moving on': that period when a young person ceases to be accommodated (or looked after) and requires support in managing this transition. This transition is much the same as that period in the life of any young person who is moving to independent living, getting a job or going off to college or university for the first time. However, for many young people who have been accommodated there are a number of other factors which need to be considered as being relevant to their circumstances, not the least of which is the fact that they have been cared for by someone else due to a number of factors mentioned elsewhere in this book, and their experiences of being looked after away from home may not have all been positive. These factors taken together create the potential for young people to feel increasingly anxious at these times and therefore enhance the chances of things going wrong for them. Furthermore, many of these young people may not have the support of their families because of the nature of their earlier experiences which led to them being accommodated. It therefore falls to the state to act in that important capacity as parent at this time. *Throughcare* refers to the preparation required for leaving care whereas *aftercare* refers to the longer-term support which may be required.

RESEARCH SUMMARY

Issues for young people moving on

Children and young people who have been accommodated tend to do less well than their contemporaries. For example, up to 75% of looked after children leave school with no formal qualifications, whilst up to 50% of young homeless people have been in the care of a local authority. Of those young people held in custody in 2000, 45% had been previously accommodated, whilst the average age for leaving care was 16/17 years old in comparison to an average age of 22 years for other young people moving to independent living (Scottish Executive 2004e).

Following recent research (Dixon and Stein 2002) and subsequent consultation by the Scottish Executive, it was agreed that young people in this situation should have access to a 'one-stop shop' where advice, guidance and assistance can be accessed swiftly and efficiently as well as being able to receive financial support if required without the complications often attached to benefit claims. The obligations of local authorities under section 29 of the Children (S) Act 1995 to support young people who are moving on have been strengthened by the provisions of section 73 of the Regulation of Care (S) Act 2001. Now, all local authorities must carry out a full assessment of need on a young person as well as developing and making available to them a system which allows them to complain about their situation or make effective representation to the local authority about the service(s) they receive. The result of this activity has been the introduction of a new framework for needs assessment and action planning for young people who have been looked after and accommodated, underpinned by new regulations and guidance (Scottish Executive 2004f) and the introduction of the 'Pathways' materials (Scottish Executive 2004g) which aims to keep the young person at the centre of the assessment and planning process in relation to their throughcare and aftercare needs. There are also new categories of eligibility in relation to the type of services available to looked after young people.

The Pathways materials have as their focus the following seven areas: lifestyle; family and friends; health and well-being; learning and work; where I live; money; and rights and legal issues. These have links to earlier LAC planning materials and the LAC review processes which allows for a more coherent approach to future planning. Key to the effectiveness of this process is the involvement of the young person themselves and their views and opinions. Practitioners need to be aware that any process is only as good as the people involved in it, so here again the utilisation of good interpersonal skills and the creation of positive relationships with the young person and other agencies are crucial to positive outcomes.

Themes and issues in caring for children and young people in substitute care

Within the literature concerning children and young people who are looked after and accommodated there are a number of key themes and issues which necessitate consideration.

The reasons behind becoming looked after

Firstly, the reasons why a child or young person has become looked after or accommodated may influence their future care and well-being. Having been the victim of abuse and neglect, for example, can leave indelible scars, literally and metaphorically. The particular history of a child or young person has a major bearing upon how they are to be cared for and what their particular support needs are likely to be. Knowing the child or young person's history is vital if effective work is to be undertaken. Never underestimate the power of history.

Mental health

Secondly, it has long been recognised and widely reported that children and young people looked after by the local authority experience higher rates of mental health difficulties both during their period of being looked after and subsequently (Buchanan 1999; Cheung and Buchanan 1997; Dimigen et al. 1999; Mather and Humphrey 1997; McCann et al. 1996; Minnis and Del Priore 2001; Quinton and Rutter 1984; Quinton et al 1998; Rowe, et al. 1984). Historically, services to meet the needs of this specific group have been delivered as part of the mainstream specialist health service to children (Child and Adolescent Mental Health Services: CAMHS), although this is now changing, with a number of local authorities having supra-specialist teams for looked after and accommodated children and young people. Some of these have mental health as a specific focus along with other issues like education and a more generalised concern with health *per se* (Butler and Vostanis 1998; Callaghan et al. 2003; Heath et al. 1994; Jackson 1989; Lehner 2003; Maclean and Gunion 2003; Minnis and Del Priore 2001; Polnay and Ward 2000; Scottish Executive 2001b).

RESEARCH SUMMARY

The mental health of young people looked after by local authorities in Scotland

The first national survey in Scotland (Meltzer et al. 2004) to look at the mental health needs of young people aged between 5 and 17 years old who were looked after by local authorities was carried out in 2002/2003. The study focused upon three types of mental health problem: conduct disorders, hyperactivity and emotional disorders. The study also aimed to consider what the impact of these disorders was in terms of social impairment for the young person as well as the social consequences of the disorder upon and for others. A third aim was to look at the effectiveness of services. The results of the study are interesting. Compared with age-related peers in ordinary households (based upon an earlier survey of the mental health needs of young people in ordinary households: Meltzer et al. 2000), those 5–10 year olds who were looked after were up to six times more likely to have a mental disorder (52% compared with 8%) whereas for the 11–15 year olds the ratio was 4:1 (41% compared with 9%).

However, research suggests that many of these services are overstretched, under-resourced and poorly structured to respond effectively to the needs of this group of children and young people (Barrows 1996; Minnis and Del Priore 2001; Nicol et al. 2000; Richardson and Joughin 2000). These factors have a range of implications for the way in which future services might be designed, with attention being focused upon how children and young people get access to these services quickly (Harman et al. 2000; Hatfield et al. 1996; Payne 2000). In this context, specialised services which address the mental health needs of looked after and accommodated children and young people are to be commended. There is some limited research available concerning the effectiveness of these specialised services and the results are promising, but more is needed (Arcelus et al. 1999) and the proposed framework for meeting children's mental health needs will hopefully remedy some of these difficulties (Scottish Executive 2005sh).

Educational performance

A third issue is that of education. Research suggests that in comparison to age-related peers, looked after and accommodated children do far worse within education. Why is this? Jackson (1987) highlighted five areas which appear to contribute to educational failure: pre-care experiences, broken schooling, low expectations, low self-esteem and a lack of continuity from caregivers.

To begin with, the experiences of children and young people prior to becoming looked after have to be taken into account. Where there are family-based problems, abuse and neglect and other difficulties, the effects of these upon the child may begin to materialise in ways which begin to show in school-based settings. For example, inability to concentrate, low self-esteem, truancy and disruptive behaviours, all of which may be symptomatic of these other difficulties, can affect educational performance. Children and young people may well bring their educational difficulties with them when they arrive in the care of the local authority. Research by Heath et al. (1989) suggests that the effects of abuse and neglect are difficult to offset in terms of their impact upon educational performance even where children are in settled placements.

Learning with care: the education of children looked after away from home by local authorities

In response to the types of concerns referred to above and as a result of the findings from a joint inspection undertaken between HMI and SWSI in 1999–2000 into the provision of social work and education services for accommodated children, the Scottish Executive launched Learning with care: the education of children looked after away from home by local authorities *(HMI/SWSI 2001). The nine recommendations arising from the inspection focus on the following areas:*

- *the need for a joint social work and educational assessment at the time a child is accommodated;*

- *quality-assurance systems are in place to ensure that statutory requirements are met in relation to looked after reviews and that appropriate information is shared concerning a child's education;*

- *all accommodated children should be in full-time education, although it was recognised that there may be exceptional cases where this is not the case;*

- *schools should ensure that all accommodated children on their roll have their learning needs identified and that a senior member of the school staff take the lead responsibility in relation to coordination and monitoring;*

- *all local authorities should develop integrated policies in relation to education and social work, with carer involvement being seen as a priority;*

- *where a child or young person continues to have contact with their parent(s), they should receive information on a regular basis regarding their child's progress, unless there are clear reasons for this not to happen;*

- *local authorities should ensure that their residential units are educationally rich;*

- *local authorities should make explicit reference to the education of accommodated children as a priority in children's services plans;*

- *local authorities should collate relevant information concerning the education of accommodated children.*

The measures referred to above, along with the requirements of associated legislation including the Education (S) Act 1980, the Children (S) Act 1995, the Standards in Scotland's Schools etc. Act 2000 and the Education (Additional Support for Learning) (S) Act 2004, are available to enhance the educational experience of all children, but the 2004 Act has particular relevance to all looked after and accommodated children and imposes new duties and powers upon all local authorities. A code of practice has been published which outlines the main provisions of the 2004 Act and makes clear what children and young people should expect to receive in terms of an educational service where there are identified additional support needs.

These initiatives have (re-) emphasised the importance of education in the lives of looked after and accommodated children.

Continuity and stability

Reference has already been made to this in relation to placements and continuity of care. It is also important to consider issues of stability and continuity of worker. Some children and young people not only experience the loss of caregivers with whom they have a relationship, but they can also lose touch with workers with whom they have positive relationships. When a child moves from one placement to another, or where even at the point of being accommodated, there may well be a change in worker. This invariably has little to do with the needs of the child or young person and more to do with the needs of the organisation. The increasing specialisation of social work related teams, multi-disciplinary or otherwise, has generally to be applauded. However, when a child's care status changes (for example, they go from being looked after at home to being accommodated), responsibility for the child will often transfer to a new worker in the specialist team. Clearly, there are arguments to support increased specialisation to meet ever-complex needs, but thought should always be given to these types of situation and the potential impact upon a child.

C H A P T E R   S U M M A R Y

This chapter has considered the arrangements that exist to care for children and young people who cannot live at home with their own families. The legal and policy context has been considered along with the importance of effective relationships underpinning good practice. We have also considered a number of specific issues which relate to the experiences of looked after/accommodated children and considered how important these are.

FURTHER READING

Clough, R (2000) *The practice of residential work.* Basingstoke: Macmillan.

A good introduction to residential work.

Long, NJ, Wood, MM and **Fecser, FA** (2001) *Life space crisis intervention: talking with students in conflict (2nd edition).* Austin TX: Pro-Ed.

An American text which takes a look at working with youngsters who are troubled. A book worth spending time with.

Chapter 6

Working together: collaboration and effective practice

Introduction

This chapter looks at the whole issue of working together with other professionals, agencies and organisations in the pursuit of ethically sound and effective practice with and for children, young people and their families. Social work with this and any other group is a very complex task and it is just not possible for one professional or indeed one agency or organisation to meet all aspects of need (Quinney 2006). This is because notions of need (Bradshaw 1972) have become more sophisticated (Sheppard and Woodcock 1999) and societal responses to these more diverse.

What is collaboration all about anyway?

What do we mean when we speak about 'collaboration'? Dictionary definitions talk about working jointly, cooperating, joining forces, teamwork, liaison, even colluding, conniving and behaving conspiratorially. I use the word here in a rather less sinister sense to include the notion of a partnership between people, agencies and organisations within the context of working towards a shared goal, however broadly defined, which involves the sharing of resources to achieve the desired outcome. Whittington (2003a) emphasises that partnerships need to exist in order that the objectives of care services can be met. Pollard et al. (2005) talk of 'inter-professional working to mean collaborative practice: that is, the process whereby members of different professions and/or agencies work together to provide integrated health and/or social care for the benefit of service users' (p10).

Take a look at the case studies below.

CASE STUDY

Mary has three children aged 2, 7 and 9 years. She is a single parent. The health visitor rang to say that Mary is not coping with the children very well. On your visit you discover the following:

- *Mary has a very low income and her child benefit has been stopped.*

- *Mary's mum has been admitted to hospital.*

- *The two older children are having difficulties at school arising in large part from problems with reading and doing homework.*

- *The flat is very cold and damp.*

- *Mary is very anxious because her ex-partner has threatened to take the children from her. Her anxieties increase when you arrive despite reassurances from the health visitor about the reason for the visit.*

Anne was born several weeks premature and has a progressive neurological disorder which means that as she grew she became less and less mobile. She also has a learning disability and suffers from epilepsy. She also self-harms and is aggressive. Within the family setting there were historical concerns surrounding the quality of care afforded to Anne's siblings over the years which had resulted in several of them being placed on the Child Protection Register. The following professionals and agencies were involved with Anne and her family over a period of years:

- *Social worker (children and families team)*
- *Social worker (learning disabilities team)*
- *Health visitor*
- *Midwife*
- *District nurse*
- *Physiotherapist*
- *GP*
- *Neurologist*
- *Occupational therapist*
- *Paediatrician*
- *Pharmacist*
- *Children's hearing*
- *Clinical psychologist*
- *Educational psychologist*
- *Police*
- *Sheriff Court*
- *Hospital staff*
- *Advocacy services*
- *Residential school staff*
- *Family centre staff*
- *Benefits agency*
- *Housing department*
- *Child support agency*
- *Voluntary organisation*
- *Community psychiatric nurse*
- *Fostering service*
- *Respite care service*

Continued ▶

- *Reflexologist*
- *Herbal therapist*
- *Massage therapist*
- *Speech and language therapist*
- *Psychotherapist*
- *Homestart*
- *Surestart*
- *Psychiatrist*

Comment

In these situations, effective collaboration is essential. However, what is the role of the social worker here? It is important to think about the overall context in order to understand the issues relating to roles and responsibilities.

In relation to Mary, the health visitor contacted you because they recognised that there were things which needed responding to that were out of their sphere of knowledge and expertise at that time. Once you have assessed the situation, you may well do the following:

- Contact the Housing Department in order that they can respond to the issue of cold and damp.
- Contact the Benefits Agency and the Child Benefit department to clarify and rectify issues concerning income.
- Offer advice on how Mary might contact the hospital to check on her mum. It might be possible to arrange for some financial assistance in relation to travel costs so that Mary can go and visit. You might arrange for some childminding if it is not possible for the children to accompany their mum to the hospital.
- Liaise with the children's school. This may lead to a referral to an educational psychologist, who might wish to assess the children in order that targeted assistance concerning their reading can be given. You might suggest that the children go to the after-school club where they could get help with their homework.
- Offer advice concerning the threats from her ex-partner and liaise with the police, particularly their domestic violence team.
- Arrange for Mary to meet with a worker from the local family centre to discuss strategies to deal with the children's behaviour.
- Arrange to see Mary again to talk about how she's feeling.

Here, the social worker collaborates and liaises with other professionals and agencies whilst aiming to empower Mary. As Payne (2005) reminds us, empowerment is about helping people 'to gain power of decision and action over their own lives' (p295). In this situation there is a clear sense of empowerment mixed with you as the worker 'taking the load' in relation to other areas. It is perhaps worth remembering that just because you could do something for Mary, it doesn't automatically mean you should. It is important to strike the right balance. Collaboration in this situation has resulted in services being provided which have improved the family's situation.

In relation to Anne, the situation is clearly much more complex, as is the rationale for collaboration. This is because there is a clear context for concern in evidence. At one level, the need for collaboration and liaison is obvious given the sheer number of services involved. It is likely that there would be some form of social work involvement in Anne's situation even in the absence of childcare concerns. The level of need is quite significant and it would be crucial to ensure that delivery was effective and well coordinated. The social worker is likely to be the key professional here, acting as the link between the service providers, a role essential in integrated children's services (Scottish Executive 2001a, 2005d). At another level, the presence of particular concerns regarding Anne's well-being above and beyond those attributable to her developmental needs makes the need for effective collaboration all the more acute. If, for example, Anne's mum were refusing to take her for necessary appointments, then your statutory responsibilities as a social worker would redefine your role. Your remit is to ensure that Anne's welfare is everyone's paramount consideration.

In this type of situation, your role may involve you as a conduit through which other professionals may consult with the family as you advocate on their behalf and there may be occasions when other professionals consult with you in relation to relevant background. These activities are all permissible so long as they occur within the context of a process involving a partnership between the family, professionals and agencies which is underpinned by respect, open and honest communication (Barrett and Keeping 2005) and a focus on the best interests of the child. Failures to do this can have disastrous consequences (Hammond 2001; Laming 2003; O'Brien et al. 2003; Reder and Duncan 1999; Reder and Duncan 2003; Sinclair and Bullock 2002; SWIA 2005; SWSI 2004).

RESEARCH SUMMARY

Regulating practice and delivering services

In terms of working together, each professional, agency and organisation is largely responsible for its own practice. All professionals deliver services in line with their own professional, agency and organisational standards, rules and protocols and regulate their practice by reference to particular ethical codes of conduct and practice standards. Such codes are integral to the professional identity of each grouping and to some extent inevitably reflect professional self-interest (Homan 1991) but they are the means through which professions formally articulate 'those distinctive attitudes which characterise the culture of a professional group' (Häring 1972, p24, cited in Butler 2002, p239). Practice standards act as a benchmark against which performance and quality can be assessed and (hopefully) assured and also operate as a means by which levels of accountability can be identified. The Scottish Social Services Council's (SSSC) Scottish Social Services Council codes of practice for social service workers and employers (2005) describe what is

Continued ▶

expected of social workers and others involved in social care. These codes have implications for everyone in terms of their conduct, both professionally and personally. Since the introduction of the Regulation of Care (S) Act 2001 and the subsequent creation of the SSSC, social care workers now have to register in order to continue to practice. This process of registration is designed to afford a measure of protection to service users by ensuring that workers are safe to practice. Similar codes exist for nurses and midwives (NMC 2002; Semple and Cable 2003), doctors (BMA 2004), psychologists (BPS 2000), teachers (GTCS 2002) and other professionals.

Analysing collaboration

When we talk of collaboration it is helpful to distinguish between the *organisational* or *agency* aspects of collaboration and the *professional* or *disciplinary* aspects. The former refers to aspects of collaboration which involve organisations and agencies within which professional and discipline-related practice takes place. Thus, the impact of the organisation, its policies, procedures, administrative practices and its general culture (Alvesson 2003) cannot and should not be overlooked. The professional or discipline aspects of collaboration are those which relate to the activities of social workers, nurses, occupational therapists and psychologists and others either individually or as members of a team. These have more of a focus upon the intra- and the inter-personal dimensions of collaboration.

A second and related distinction is that which refers to the level of integration, interaction, adaptation and flexibility between the organisational and professional dimensions. In the language of collaboration, there are two main prefixes in use; 'multi' and 'inter'. We have multi-agency practice/teams/collaboration, multi-disciplinary meetings, multi-professional forums, etc.; we also have inter-agency practice, inter-agency collaboration, inter-disciplinary teamwork, and so on. The prefix 'multi' tends to represent situations and arrangements where the agencies, teams and professionals tend to work alongside and in parallel to each other without dismantling professional boundaries or professional identities. The prefix 'inter' tends to denote a more integrative, interactive and adaptive arrangement which (theoretically) allows for a much easier partnership where organisations and individual professionals are (more) comfortable with the transfer of knowledge, values and skills between organisational and professional boundaries, thus maximising the free flow of ideas, skill mix and the development of creative practices (Payne 2000). In reality these two terms are often used interchangeably and within any team or organisational setting there are likely to be variations on the theme and many shades of grey.

ACTIVITY 6.1

Refer back to the case study above concerning Anne and her family. Under the following headings, try to identify which of the following are represented in the list:

- *organisations;*
- *agencies;*
- *professions;*
- *disciplines.*

In compiling your list, you might have come up with the following:

- Organisations: local authority; National Health Service; Health Board; Court Service; private organisations; voluntary organisations; police; Scottish Children's Hearing Administration.

- Agencies: social work; hospital; community health (GPs, district nurses); education; psychological services; benefits agency; child support; police services; voluntary agencies; private agencies (reflexology, herbal).

- Professions: social work; nursing; teaching; psychology; medicine; administration; speech and language therapy; psychotherapy; physiotherapy; pharmacy; legal.

- Disciplines: child and family social work; learning disabilities social work; health visiting; children's reporter; community midwifery; (paediatric) physiotherapy; neurology; educational psychology; clinical psychology, (paediatric) pharmacology; residential social work.

The distinctions between these categories can at times be somewhat artificial and what is and is not a profession is a debate which has raged forever and not one we shall enter into here (Flexner 1915/2001; Payne 1996).

The basis for and the context of collaboration

This specialisation brings with it its own challenges, not the least of which is how they work and fit together to make sure that need is effectively and efficiently met.

As we saw in Chapter 1, the whole issue of working together was first raised in the professional arena in the post-war years when it became apparent that the nature of many of the difficulties experienced by children, young people and their families were often interrelated. The nature of family life is multi-faceted and increasingly complex and as a social worker in the 21st century your skills are as much about direct work with other professionals, their agencies and organisations as they are about direct work with children, young people and their families. You must be able to use your communication and interpersonal skills (Koprowska 2005; Thompson 2002, 2003) to work effectively and efficiently with a wide range of other professionals whose knowledge, skills and values are crucial to achieving the task (Horwarth and Shardlow 2003). With ever-changing conceptions of need and increasingly complex demands, achieving the broad task with children, young people and their families is no longer the sole preserve of social work, although as Chapter 7 will show, there are a number of important (reserved) functions which social workers are still best placed to carry out.

Influences upon collaborative practice

The following sections consider a number of interrelated contexts which influence the nature of collaboration. These are:

- the legal and policy context;

- the organisational and agency context;

- the personal and professional context;

- the practice context;

- the higher education and learning context (Whittington 2003b).

To some extent these categorisations are artificial in that they may appear to draw distinctions which do not exist in pure form and there will be overlap between them. However, it is useful to consider these areas separately in order that the main themes and issues of each can be highlighted.

The legal and policy context

The current legislative and policy context is one which has collaboration as a key theme. This emphasis on collaborative practice recognises that no one organisation or agency or any one professional group or discipline is able to successfully deliver the range of services required in the 21st century. Legislation and policy are now designed to facilitate collaborative working and this has been influenced by a number of factors, including:

- the changing nature of need and the way it is defined, and by whom (Scottish Executive 2005j);

- changing and ever-increasing demands upon human services and increasing specialisation;

- the impact of 'near misses', child fatalities and the subsequent inquiries into these (Axford and Bullock 2005; Bostock et al. 2005; Reder et al. 1993; Sinclair and Bullock 2002);

- an increasing recognition of the need to address the whole person in terms of how services are designed and delivered (Bronfenbrenner 1979; Clode 2003; Department of Health 2000);

- service user perspectives (Beresford 2002; Cleaver and Freeman 1995; Dale 2004; Statham 2004);

- accountability issues (OPM/CIPFA 2004);

- issues concerning the nature of professional identity, training and development (Barr 2003; Miller et al. 2001);

- issues concerning the boundaries between individuals, professionals, agencies and organisations including communication issues (Reder and Duncan 2003; Tietze Cohen and Musson 2003; Woodhouse and Pengelly 1991)

- awareness of organisational influences (Alvesson 2003; Hudson 1987, 2002);

- the nature of working in groups (teams) (Øvretveit et al. 1997; Payne 2000).

Legislation, policy and guidance therefore offer a framework within which collaboration can take place.

Section 21 of the 1995 Act places upon local authorities the option of requesting of others, notably 'any other local authority', 'a health board', 'a national health service trust' and/or 'any person authorised by the Secretary of State' (s.21(2)) for 'help in the exercise of their functions' (s.21(1)). This forms the legal basis for collaborative working between professionals, agencies and organisations under the 1995 Act and when such a request is made by the local authority, those so requested have a duty to comply. However, there is a caveat which refers to those requested as having to comply only if the request made is compatible with their own statutory or other duties and obligations. This of course makes perfect sense in most cases; for example, it would be inappropriate for a local authority to request that the health board provide a family with a house. But, what about those situations where an authority requests of the education department that a place be provided for a child but they say they do not have such a place available? Should the education department create a *new* resource? And what if they feel they can't because there is no money? These and other ethical dilemmas are very real and are likely to be faced by you and your colleagues at some point.

Collaboration takes place at a number of different levels, including:

- *The policy level*: policy-makers from different government departments, other agencies and organisations collaborate to develop policies which reflect the optimum way of meeting social need.

- *The strategic level*: agencies and organisations collaborate to design, develop and finance services from joint resources in order to implement the policies.

- *The organisational/managerial level*: agencies and organisations collaborate to determine how the strategy for service delivery should be implemented and who should be accountable and responsible for this.

- *The operational level*: professionals, agencies and organisations collaborate to implement services 'on the ground', looking at the practicalities of making things happen. This includes thinking about how long it takes to do a particular piece of work and who is best placed to do it in the here and now.

- *The practice level*: this is where practitioners collaborate with colleagues both in their own and other teams to provide those services so designed directly to the people they are working with.

These levels represent the broad spread of activity within the service arena; there are other ways of representing this (Whittington 2003b) but these offer a straightforward way of appreciating that collaboration takes place in a range of contexts at a number of different levels and is very much a necessity.

In terms of specific policy direction regarding working together, the area of childcare and protection is one replete with guidance and exhortations to collaborate. Given the complex nature of this area of work it is not surprising that much has been said about the necessity of close collaboration between professionals, agencies and their organisations. The policy document *Protecting children: a shared responsibility* (Scottish Office 1998) reminds us that:

> *A number of statutory agencies and voluntary organisations assist children in a variety of ways. Dealing with child abuse is not, however, the preserve of any one public or voluntary service. If they are to protect children effectively, they must collaborate closely. (p1)*

It then goes on to set out the principles seen to underpin effective inter-agency collaboration in child protection situations. Such guidance is designed to offer clear advice to practitioners as to how all those involved in child protection should work together, delineating the responsibilities of respective agencies in terms of the management of such situations (see Chapter 4).

RESEARCH SUMMARY

Recommendations from the Child Protection Audit and Review relating to inter-agency collaboration

- *All agencies should review their procedures to ensure that practitioners have access to the right information at the right time.*

- *Through the Child Protection Committees, all agencies should improve access to help for children who have been abused and neglected.*

- *Standards of practice should be drawn up against which all services should audit their services.*

- *The remit of the Child Protection Committees should be revised.*

- *The mechanisms for the dissemination of information about child abuse and neglect should be strengthened.*

- *Agency resources should be pooled.*

- *A new approach should be developed for tackling risks.*

- *Computer-based information systems should be developed to include a single integrated assessment.*

- *Minimum standards of professional knowledge and competence for child protection workers should be clarified.*

- *Undertake another review in three years' time.*

(Scottish Executive 2002e, pp13–16)

At a broader level, there are a range of primary statutes and other policy documents which specifically refer to, actively promote or otherwise facilitate collaboration between professionals, agencies and organisations. These are noted in the box below.

RESEARCH SUMMARY

Legislation and policy for collaboration
- *Social Work (S) Act 1968*

- *Education (S) Act 1980*

- *National Health Service and Community Care Act 1990*

- *Children (S) Act 1995*

Continued

- *Local Government in Scotland Act 2003*
- *Protecting Children – A Shared Responsibility (1998)*
- *Aiming for Excellence (1999)*
- *New Community Schools (1998)*
- *Social Inclusion Strategy (1999)*
- *Sure Start (1998)*
- *Community Care: A Joint Future (2000)*
- *Towards a Healthier Scotland (2000)*
- *Changing Children's Services Fund (2001)*
- *For Scotland's Children (2001)*
- *Promoting Children's Mental Health within Early Years and School Settings (2001)*
- *Regulation of Care (S) Act 2001*
- *Community Care and Health (S) Act 2002*
- *Community Care (Joint Working etc.) Regulations 2002*
- *It's Everyone's Job to Make Sure I'm Alright (2002)*
- *Caleb Ness Inquiry (2003)*
- *Getting Our Priorities Right (2003)*
- *Integrated Strategy for Early Years (2003)*
- *The Laming Inquiry (2003)*
- *Making It Work for Scotland's Children (2003)*
- *Mental Health (Care and Treatment) (S) Act 2003*
- *Protection of Children (S) Act 2003*
- *Anti-Social Behaviour etc. (S) Act 2004*
- *Education (Additional Support for Learning) (S) Act 2004*
- *Framework for Standards (2004)*
- *Guidance for Integrated Children's Services Plans (2004)*
- *Guidance on Local Authority Accountability (2004)*
- *Hidden Harm (2004)*
- *National Health Service Reform (S) Act 2004*
- *21st Century Review of Social Work (2004/05)*
- *Community Planning (2005)*

All of these statutes and policy documents make provision for collaboration, cooperation and partnership at a number of different levels. This provision is either prescriptive, as in the 1995 Act, or facilitative, as in the provisions of many of those policy documents referred to.

However, the many exhortations to work together, as exemplified by many of the recommendations contained within inquiry reports, do not always bring about the desired results (Hudson 2002). Below we shall look at some of those factors which make collaboration a reality or not. If we ignore the broader contextual factors which relate to collaboration, then we are very likely to continue to wonder why it doesn't work, because sometimes it doesn't. Therefore, being alive to those factors which may help or hinder the collaborative process is a necessary part of the collaborative endeavour itself.

The agency and organisational context

As a social worker (or teacher, nurse, psychologist, etc.) we work within an organisational context. Organisations have their own rules and regulations which govern their functioning and are designed primarily to ensure their continued existence. Social work exists within an organisational context which may or may not be fully aligned to the same value base. For example, as a social worker you may be employed by an organisation which is profit-driven. A situation may arise where you feel, as a professional social worker, that a particular course of action is necessary. The organisation, on the other hand, believes that this will be too costly and affect profits. You are therefore prevented from undertaking this piece of work. In a local authority social work department, you may similarly believe that a child requires a particular resource but are told that this is not available as the budget is overspent. Another example may be where an external organisation to whom your agency relates to in a professional context requires that you produce reports for them within certain specified timescales. Your professional view may be that such a timescale, whilst not impossible to meet, is somewhat unrealistic as any report produced in such a timescale would not be sufficiently detailed to do full justice to what may well be a very complex situation. The era of performance indicators is upon us and many workers are heard across the country bemoaning the fact that quantity appears to be what managers and policy-makers are interested in rather than quality. These are the kinds of conflicts which can arise when the organisational and professional contexts appear to clash.

In a similar way, there are situations which arise where the agency may adopt particular administrative or operational requirements which appear to constrain professional judgement and practice. It may be the case that in order for you as a member of one organisation to obtain a resource from another organisation (let's say in the form of staff time from another professional), you have to make numerous formal requests, in writing, via your manager, who correspondingly requests this from your colleagues' manager. This can take time and it can be frustrating, particularly in those situations where the time you require is minimal and the professional whose time you would like is happy to oblige and yet cannot because their organisational and related administrative systems prohibit this in the absence of signed authorisations, which are sent to the finance department for cost analysis in relation to unit costs per head for inter-agency collaboration. Here again, at the organisational level such practices are completely understandable, but from the professional perspective, absolutely maddening.

What effect might these kinds of organisational issues have upon effective collaboration? Both intra- and inter-organisational collaboration depends upon the degree of fit between organisational goals and professional goals. These are not always in perfect accord and the resultant tensions can at times be debilitating, particularly in high-stress situations where professionals simply want to get on with the job in hand rather than becoming embroiled in administrative processes which at times appear to have little or nothing to do with supporting children, young people and their families. Believe me, I have been there! It may be that in response to these tensions, professionals may adopt a particular approach to practice which may be defensive, routinised, defeatist or otherwise dangerous (Thompson 2005). However, if the organisation is sensitive enough and good-quality supervision is available to the worker, then these issues can be discussed and effectively dealt with.

The issue to recognise is that organisations have their own 'rules of engagement' and these may not always appear to be synchronous with the values of the profession in terms of ongoing practice. The social worker in these situations will have to utilise their own communication and interpersonal skills to the full and engage with the organisation on behalf of their client in an advocacy role. Thompson (2005) makes the point that most social workers have as their practice-focus direct work with individuals, in this case children, young people and their families. What is not so readily acknowledged, nor indeed readily attended to, particularly in qualifying training, is that an increasing amount of time is spent in direct work with organisations, agencies and other professionals. Thus, the needs of the organisation and its service delivery networks demand a significant amount of effort on the part of the individual professional. These skills we shall consider below. However, what does need to be acknowledged is that the organisational context has a pervasive influence on the practice of professionals and as such must be accounted for in relation to conceptions of day-to-day social work practice.

These factors are often to the fore in today's social work arena because of the tendency for services to 'reorganise' on a regular basis. In the drive to integrate services for the benefit of users, services have had to realign themselves with different partners and stakeholders as the requirements for increasingly specialised, responsive and accountable services have taken hold. Policy initiatives, different funding options and new categories of need all conspire to place demands upon existing services to be more effective and efficient. Competition, once the watchword of private, 'for-profit' organisations is now a central feature of the human service lexicon, particularly insofar as third-sector (voluntary) organisations are concerned. Whilst these organisations are 'not-for-profit', their very existence can often be threatened by other organisations competing for core and short-term funding to provide services from both central government and local authorities. These economic drivers mean that when a service reconfigures or otherwise reinvents itself, fragmentation can occur, leaving both service users and professionals confused and bewildered. Many funding streams are relatively short-term, often for three years, at which point the new service has to be self-funding or otherwise financed through core funding. The effect on professionals can be quite debilitating, especially if your job is on the line at the end of a funding period.

These issues are very much to the fore in terms of the current situation in childcare practice in all parts of the UK. Whilst policy would endeavour to generate a climate within which collaboration and cooperation can flourish to the advantage of service users, the interface between policy intent, organisational *raison d'être* and professional obligation is often blurred and somewhat jagged at the edges. Hudson (1987) notes that there are two main difficulties for organisations when faced with the need to collaborate, as most social welfare organisations these days are expected to. Firstly, the organisation faces the loss of its freedom to act independently, having to relinquish control over its own domain. Secondly, and very importantly in relation to the current welfare climate, it has to invest scarce resources into developing and maintaining collaborative relationships. From an organisational perspective, the investment in collaboration may in fact not yield any benefits. However, it is also the case that just such an investment may in fact increase the capacity for it to achieve its goals because it can then utilise the resources of the other organisation(s) and thereby achieve a state of interdependence.

The personal and professional context

At the individual level there are a number of issues to consider which relate to the whole area of collaborative activity. Motivation is a key factor in terms of how well people work, both alone and as part of a team (Herzberg 1968). Being part of a team implies many things, not the least of which is that the team will function effectively. Notions of teams and team-working are contested issues (Øvretveit 1997; Payne 2000) and some of these have been referred to above. Payne and others refer to teams and to work groups, the former having some sense of identity, a shared vision, clarity concerning role, task and function and a range of shared policy statements on key service areas, whilst the latter work group is seen as being more diffuse, less focused and formed for a very short period to undertake a specific piece of work before being disbanded. Both of these arrangements exist within the context of collaborative working in social work, as do variations on this theme and groupings which may lie somewhere in between.

Whatever the particular arrangement, it is important to realise that teams are subject to particular dynamics and go through a number of processes in their development. These processes reflect human capabilities and issues and can determine whether the group will function effectively or not. Tuckman and Jensen (1977) describe a four-stage process:

- *Forming (socialisation)*: During this stage of coming together, the key issues will relate to the communication of team objectives, orientation and socialisation. This 'forming' stage is likely to be very unproductive in terms of task-related activity, although this stage is crucial to the overall process. In fact, the 'forming' stage is best accomplished without there being too many task demands made upon the team. It is important to note that if this stage is not given enough time, then the next stage, that of 'storming', may last longer than it should, which could be detrimental to the whole team process and the achievement of its objectives.

  Essentially the 'forming' stage is concerned with the development of social relations, the exchange of professional and personal information and the breaking down of barriers. It is in many respects characterised by 'sizing up' the other members and of getting a sense of the knowledge, skills and values of others which allows for people to judge their position within the group. It is also important to note that the presence of a team leader is important at this stage; otherwise there may well be no movement forward and the 'self-selection' of a leader may create difficulties.

- *Storming (conflict):* This is the stage where team members are beginning to get to know each other. This can be the most difficult and worrying time in the life of the group. In some cases it may seem that the team is rife with internal conflict, disagreement and discord and may in fact give the impression of being on the verge of collapse. The team leader is crucial here, for if these differences and tensions are well managed, with a clear focus on why the group is in existence, then it is likely that the group will emerge strong and well developed with a very clear sense of its collective identity.

- *Norming (rule-setting):* In this stage, the group develops its working structures and clarifies its internal and external relationships. Roles are established and clarified with everyone being expected to sign up to these. Agreement is reached on how conflicts will be dealt with and the theme is one of a search for consensus. It is this phase which allows for people to relax and begin to focus upon the task at hand, bringing to bear on the situation the very things they brought to the group: their unique contribution of knowledge, values and skills.

- *Performing (doing):* Once the rules have been set and the task defined, the team can get on with the work. This stage is characterised by high task orientation.

These four phases are adequate to explain most aspects of team formation and performance. However, some writers feel that this typology is somewhat limited and have added other stages (Cartwright 2002):

- *Dorming (plateau):* In this stage, the team has been working well but suddenly reaches a plateau where performance levels fall off. This may represent nothing more than a team functioning at its maximum level. If there is no more potential to be had from the team, then there is, arguably, not a problem. However, if it appears to be the case that the team is not achieving its objectives, despite what appears to be maximum performance, then there is a problem. It might be that some team members have given up on the team and feel they have no more to contribute, or perhaps internal conflicts and tensions are compromising the productivity of the team. Whatever the cause, it has to be dealt with. If, however, the team is performing at its maximum and running smoothly, it is important not to perceive the apparent lack of energy and the dynamism of earlier periods as problematic. If it isn't broken, don't try to fix it.

- *Re-forming:* This stage recognises that most groups will change their membership at some time for a number of reasons. Some of these will relate to personal reasons, some will relate to the wider needs of the parent organisation(s) or a change in task orientation. Whatever the case, and it is very likely that every team in the UK has altered its membership at some time during its existence, new members alter the established dynamic. As a result, there is a period where the group needs to re-establish itself because of the new member(s) who bring with them different characteristics, knowledge, values and skills which need to be worked into the fabric of the group. Mini-phases of forming, storming and norming can be seen to occur. These can be perceived as being indicative of problems within the group but they are nothing more than the team re-establishing social relations, positions and rules in respect of the new members. It has to be remembered that in these situations, a drop in team performance is likely until equilibrium is restored.

- *Adjourning:* Some teams are permanent; an area social work team is likely to be there for a long time. However, some teams are not permanent, either by design or default. If a team is established on the basis that it is not going to be permanent, then this needs to be stated at the outset so that people can concentrate on achieving the task rather than on diversionary activities designed to prolong something which has to end. These kinds of activities are fully understandable but much energy and effort can be wasted and hopes built up only to be shattered. When a team adjourns, this is likely to be difficult for some people as the relationships they have developed may be very significant to them and so they may be grieving for these losses as they can have an impact upon one's sense of self and both personal and professional identity. This phase has to be managed effectively; endings must be recognised and feelings of loss acknowledged.

In the face of political pressure to collaborate, more and more groups or teams are formed on a frequent basis. Group dynamics play a central role in determining how likely effective collaboration will be so it is important that attention is paid to this aspect of collaborative practice.

Professional identity and collaboration

Having a clear sense of professional identity is generally regarded as a vital ingredient to effective practice, irrespective of the discipline concerned or the location of that within a particular agency or organisational context. Knowing what it is you do as a social worker, a nurse, a teacher, doctor or physiotherapist is pretty important to service users. This identity will reflect differing knowledge bases, theoretical orientations, value bases, skill levels and a range of other factors often unique to that profession. These differences must be seen constructively and recognition given to the value of diversity.

The practice context

By far the most important aspect of collaboration is that between the worker(s) and those children, young people and their families with whom they have contact. It is important to recognise that the very nature of the intervention itself may help or hinder the sense of collaboration, cooperation and partnership experienced. For example, in cases where the client is in some respects involuntary, there may be resistance to all aspects of work, and cooperation and collaboration may well not be evident (Trotter 1999). By 'involuntary' I refer to those individuals who may actually be or feel that they are being compelled to work with you against their will. Where a child has been removed from the family against their wishes, the parent may have to work with you in order to have the child returned to their care. Where a young person has been offending, they may have been directed by the children's hearing to attend a group which has as its focus the reduction of offending behaviour. The young person may only attend because they know that not to do so might have more serious consequences (for example, detention in secure accommodation), whilst the parent referred to above may only cooperate because not to do so reduces the likelihood of the child being returned home. In these situations partnership, cooperation and collaboration may well be principles furthest from people's minds and as a result the demands upon the workers' communication and interpersonal skills become that much greater.

From the perspective of what inquiries and reports have told us, there are a number of issues which appear to emerge time after time which relate to the whole issue of collaboration and why at times it appears to be problematic. When we speak of collaboration, we imply that its many facets are operating seamlessly. If collaboration is to happen then its constituent elements need to be evident. Some of these are:

- effective communication;
- adequate sharing of information;
- accurate recording of information;
- understanding of roles and responsibilities;
- clarity of purpose;
- clear timeframes;
- effective decision-making;
- easy access to and effective use of resources.

The nature of practice has therefore to include these things as well as the human elements referred to above.

The educational context

In relation to the educational context, I refer specifically to the need for those institutions of higher education which provide qualifying and post-qualifying training for social work and social care staff, as well as continuous professional and employee development courses, to actively include reference to collaborative working within the curriculum. The Standards in Social Work Education in Scotland (Scottish Executive 2003a) make reference to the need for students of social work to be able to work effectively within organisations and to work collaboratively. These are addressed by all institutions but there is a need for the explicit juxtapositioning of those transferable skills to the notion referred to above concerning social workers spending significant amounts of time in direct work with organisations.

A further development is that relating to inter-professional education (Barr 2003; Miller et al. 2001) which recognises the need for students in a range of professions to learn together with other professionals from the very start of their careers, and also whilst in practice.

At the practice level, many groups (for example, child protection committees) are concerned to offer training to staff from different professions, agencies and organisations who contribute in some way to service provision for children, young people and their families. This endeavour extends not only to a range of different and diverse professional groups, but also to the social care community and the community at large.

What is clear is that the need to work together has never been more acute than it is today. It is therefore essential that policy-makers, managers, practitioners and educators appreciate what collaboration actually entails and approach it systematically, applying theory and critical analysis to it rather than assuming that effective collaboration just happens. Like most things in life, it has to be worked at and not taken for granted.

Areas where collaboration takes place

In working with children, young people and their families, collaboration is needed with a range of professionals, agencies and organisations (Quinney 2006). As we saw in the case study concerning Anne and her family, there can be an almost limitless number of potential collaborators who are able to provide needed services. In simplistic terms, what is required needs to be provided. That, however, has the potential to raise a whole set of new difficulties, not the least of which are those which relate to relevance, quality, accountability, confidentiality, cost and coordination. I shall consider each of these in turn. However, before we look at these it is perhaps helpful to think about those organisations, agencies and professionals who are most likely to provide services to children, young people and their families. Some of these are noted in the box below. But this is not an exhaustive list. See if you can add any to the list.

- Health: *GPs; nurses; community nurses; community psychiatric nurses; health visitors; midwives; psychiatrists; physiotherapists; occupational therapists; speech and language therapists; paediatricians; clinical psychologists; dieticians; health promotion workers.*

- Education: *teachers; teaching assistants; educational psychologists; new community school staff; community education workers.*

- Housing: *housing officers; support staff.*

- Specialists: *substance misuse workers; alcohol misuse workers; criminal justice workers; domestic violence workers; psychotherapists; family therapists; psychologists; counsellors; youth workers; voluntary organisations; self-help groups.*

- Police; *reporter to the children's panel; Sheriff Courts.*

Quality and safety

All of these people may well offer a service at some point. The breadth of service provision is quite breathtaking today. These are valuable assets within society and they need to be nurtured and developed to ensure maximum benefit for all. But they also need to be regulated and quality-assured. The children, young people and their families you will be working with are some of the most vulnerable people in society. As a result, we all have a responsibility to ensure that the services available are safe, effective, cost-effective, easily and readily accessible, responsive and relevant.

In Scotland, the Social Work Inspection Agency (SWIA) exists to do just this along with Her Majesty's Inspectorate of Education (HMIe) and its Services for Children Unit, the Care Commission, Her Majesty's Inspectorate of Constabulary (HMIC) and NHS Quality Improvement Scotland (QIS). Audit tools are used to check whether services are 'best value' and evaluations take place which look at their effectiveness in promoting change and enhancing welfare (see Local Government in Scotland Act 2003). There are also a range of national standards which we have referred to throughout the preceding chapters. These standards offer a benchmark against which services can be checked.

Relevance

Any service needs to be relevant for the people at whom it is aimed. If you are putting together a care package for a child you must be clear that it is relevant to their needs; too much intrusion is indicative of poor practice and a lack of respect for the child's privacy and self-determination. Conversely, too little involvement may mean that needs are not being met. Balance is the key and this should be assisted and underpinned by reference to a thorough assessment and clearly defined criteria relating to what any identified service needs to do and for how long. Good social work skills relating to assessment, planning, intervention, review and evaluation are critical.

Accountability

The issues of quality have been referred to above, but it is also important here to refer to accountability. All service providers are accountable to service users for the quality of the service they provide. You have a professional responsibility to ensure that your practice is ethically sound and does not oppress or discriminate in any way. You as the worker are accountable to the service user, your employer and your professional body (the SSSC).

Confidentiality

In terms of confidentiality, the more people that are involved, the more likely it is that confidentiality could be breached. There are of course clear guidelines on when it is permissible to breach the rules of confidentiality and these relate primarily to those situations where there is a threat to life or where a person is at risk of harm (Cordess 2001). In more general situations, if there are several agencies involved in providing services this means that information has to be shared with more and more people. In the normal course of events you would advise the child and their family that you need to pass on information to whoever it might be in order that they can assess whether the service they have on offer is actually relevant. In most cases, this will be acceptable. However, in some cases you may have opposition and in these circumstances you have to decide whether the sharing of information is likely to cause unnecessary harm to someone or whether not to do so is likely to compromise the welfare of the child. In cases of suspected child abuse and neglect, the sharing of relevant information to relevant parties is explicitly accepted as good practice providing that people are told that this is/has and will continue to happen where there are concerns for the welfare of a child. New proposals concerning the sharing of information are currently being discussed within the Scottish Executive and form part of the review of children's services in Scotland at this time (Scottish Executive 2005d).

Coordination

Coordination is an essential part of effective service delivery. The more services there are in place for a child or young person, the greater the need for effective coordination. In child protection cases, an inter-agency child protection plan will be available to map out the respective roles and responsibilities of all those to be involved with the child and the family. This plan is reviewed on a regular basis and requires for its effective implementation clear and effective communication between all involved. In situations which may well be as complex, but not as dangerous, a similar plan can be drawn up locally. You as the social worker for the child would have the responsibility of clarifying with all concerned what their particular role would be and of delineating timescales for the completion of certain tasks. From you this demands good workload management skills, the ability to organise yourself and other people as well as the ability to challenge and confront people when things seem to be slipping. Here, again, good communication and interpersonal skills are crucial. Within the review of children's services referred to above and the *21st century social work review* (Scottish Executive 2005j), the role of the social worker as the key professional in relation to organisation and coordination is being considered.

C H A P T E R   S U M M A R Y

This chapter has considered the issue of working with other people in order to ensure that services are delivered effectively to children, young people and their families. No longer is collaboration something we might think about doing if we have the time; it is central to the social work task and good communication and interpersonal skills, along with an understanding of the nature of group dynamics, are important prerequisites for effective collaboration at all levels.

FURTHER READING

Barrett, **G**, **Sellman**, **D and Thomas**, **J** (eds) (2005) *Interprofessional working in health and social care: professional perspectives*. Basingstoke: Palgrave Macmillan.

A useful text which offers a coherent account of some of the issues involved in collaborative working.

Horwarth, **J and Shardlow**, **S** (2003) *Making links across specialisms: understanding modern social work practice*. Lyme Regis: Russell House.

A very useful text which has as its focus some of the complexities of collaboration within and across specialist areas of practice.

Woodhouse, **D and Pengelly**, **P** (1991) *Anxiety and the dynamics of collaboration*. Aberdeen: Aberdeen University Press.

A classic exposition from a psychodynamic perspective of some of the human issues involved in collaborative working.

Quinney, **A** (2006) *Collaborative social work practice*. Exeter: Learning Matters.

A text which looks at collaborative working with a range of professional groupings.

Chapter 7

Twenty-first-century social work in Scotland

Introduction

This chapter will take a brief look at where we have been and where we might be going in Scotland in terms of social work in general, and what the future might hold for social work with children, young people and their families in particular. This does not mean that we have to rely on a crystal ball to get a sense of what might be; rather, we need to look at what has been, what is now and, on the basis of that, what ought to be for the future. I deliberately say 'ought to be' because I feel that it is important that we maintain a sense of pragmatism within our thinking; 'wish-lists' are one thing but reality can sometimes be something entirely different. And it is very important to understand that there are many competing agendas and other influences in operation which impact upon the capacity of societies to respond exactly as everyone would want them to in relation to issues appertaining to need.

Where have we been?

Social work has its roots in the ethos of caring, with early Victorian philanthropy providing its initial infrastructure through charitable and religious organisational structures. As industrialisation developed, the state became increasingly aware of its need to provide services to the most needy and vulnerable. Some would argue (Clarke 1993) that the basis for such state involvement arose from the need to support the capitalist ruling classes by ensuring the (potential) workforce was healthy, educated, housed and reasonably well controlled, with the care of children by their parents being an essentially vicarious activity designed to provide a healthy and competent workforce in perpetuity. Others would argue that social work developed in response to the apparent failings of industrialisation and urbanisation, thereby reflecting an inherently humanist concern for others and their condition.

As social work and social care have developed, there have been a number of phases through which they have passed which have themselves been representative of particular social philosophies and discourses dominant at any given time (see Chapters 1 and 3). These have had an influence on social work practice as well as upon the thinking which surrounds it in terms of its *raison d'être* and, like all professions, social work needs to evolve with the times. Times change and as a result the responses to those in need must also change. Social work practice is inextricably bound to change and the reality is that there will always be people in need of help and support. Most of us are fortunate enough to be in the position of having family and friends around us to help us through difficult times. There are many who are not so fortunate and have to rely on the comfort of strangers to assist them in meeting their needs. The most vulnerable people in society are often those with whom social workers have the most contact, many of these being undervalued within society (Wilkes 1981). Some people, particularly children and young people, may have family around them but be in a position where those people are the very source of the threat or danger itself. In circumstances like these their reliance on strangers may well be absolute. This is a (social) fact of life (Searle 1995). Social life is complicated and, as Adams et al. (2005) note:

> Social work is about human beings in their social worlds. Human beings are complex in themselves and we live in complicated worlds. Social work practice, therefore, is challenging because it constantly requires dealing with complexity. (p1)

The social worlds we all inhabit are unique to each of us and are created by us, for us and with us in our interactions with others as well as in response to our interactions with ourselves and the world at large (Berger and Luckman 1979; Searle 1995). Social workers need to be attuned to this and it is important that their responses are reflexive and not simply reactive. The same goes for the responses of services of which the individual social worker is a part. Services need to be in tune with society and the people within it. As a result it is important for social work to be very clear about what it does, why it does it, how it does it, who it does it for and whether it is the best placed profession to do 'it' at all for anyone? The question also arises as to what it is that social work actually does: what is its unique contribution? (Scottish Executive 2005o).

These and other questions lie at the heart of social work because if the profession is to continue to meet need effectively, then it has to ensure that it continues to do it well. If we think back to Chapter 1 we will recall how the Social Work (S) Act 1968 was one of the first statutes to recognise that services needed not only to respond to need, but that they should actively seek to identify it and respond appropriately (s.12). This forward thinking epitomises Scottish social work practice. Recently, these and a range of other questions have been the subject of debate and enquiry within Scotland through the 21st Century Social Work Review (www.21csocialwork.org.uk) which sought to address the issues facing social work and other related public, voluntary and private services which have a role to play in creating a transformational social work which 'addresses people's lives as they are now and helps them to change in such a way that enhances their social relationships and well-being both now and in the future' (Adams 2005, p2). Whilst this may appear to represent an essentially individualistic view of the focus for transformational social work, we should not forget that individual action is the precursor to collective action and socio-structural change. Thus, this is entirely consistent with the social inclusion agenda and the need to dismantle and remove barriers to effective and harmonious social relationships. It is also worth noting that the review looked at a range of services which are seen as being complementary to social work and its task, particularly as we remember that social work aims to see the whole person. Therefore, the relevance of other services such as health and education are seen in the context of how these contribute to the overall well-being of the person, which is at the core of social work's concern and reflects what Sewpaul (2005) sees as part of the task of 're-inscribing social work into civil society' (p211).

Where are we going? Social work in the 21st century

What is different about social work in the 21st century? The answer to that lies in the fact that, as we have said before, society is changing rapidly and there is a need to ensure that social work services are in tune with all of this. Lishman (2005) refers to a range of 'political, social and demographic drivers' (p1) which have and continue to force change across and within the public sector due largely to the fact that 'the geo-social landscape has altered since the creation of the welfare state and social care services need to be designed and delivered to meet the needs of *contemporary* society' (emphasis added) (ibid). Lishman goes on to suggest that 'social work seems to be moving from an era of "deserving" and "welfare" to "empowerment" and "well-being" (with) business principles being applied to the public sector' (ibid).

The White Paper *Aiming for excellence* (Scottish Executive 1999) is perhaps the earliest indicator of the increased awareness within Scotland of the need for social work and social care services to be and remain responsive to service user need whilst being reliable, efficiently and effectively delivered and built around best practice. These essential principles formed the vision for the future of social work services and formed the basis of the White Paper and essentially began a lengthy review of social work which has culminated in some respects with the report of the 21st Century Social Work Review Group, *Changing lives* (Scottish Executive 2006a). Along the way, there have been several significant inquiries and reviews of differing aspects of social work and social care which have had to take into account the cross-cutting nature of the social work task itself. Some of these (O'Brien et al. 2003; SWSI 2004) have effectively led to a situation where public and political confidence in social work has been threatened. It had therefore become necessary for social work to look at itself more critically. Inquiries into particular situations can and do have positive consequences with regard to 'lessons to be learned'. However, the complexities of modern living and social works' continued capacity to respond as effectively as possible in this changing world were seen as something requiring considerable thought. In doing this it has become increasingly obvious that there is a need to document the inter-connectedness between the policies which exist to address need of many sorts and at many different levels in a variety of ways. The complexity of contemporary society is mir-rored by the complexity of policy. The box below offers a number of links which will highlight cross-cutting themes in social work and social care as well as key policy docu-ments in relation to health and community care, criminal justice and children, young people and their families, the three main areas considered by the review group.

RESEARCH SUMMARY

Useful web links

Cross-cutting social services issues:
www.scotland.gov.uk/Topics/Education/social-care-social-work/Cross-cuttingIssues/
PolicyDocuments

Health and community care:
www.scotland.gov.uk/Topics/People/Social-Inclusion/19953/21078

Criminal justice:
www.scotland.gov.uk/Topics/People/Social-Inclusion/19952/21079

Children, young people and their families:
www.scotland.gov.uk/Topics/People/Social-Inclusion/19951/21081

Policy map of key documents:
www.scotland.gov.uk/resource/doc/1135/0010034.pdf

The 21st century social work review

The review was initiated by Scottish ministers in June 2004 with six broad objectives:

- to clearly define the role and purpose of social workers and the social work profession;

- to identify improvements in the organisation and delivery of social work services;

- to develop a strong quality improvement framework and culture, supported by robust inspection;

- to strengthen leadership and management, giving clear direction to the service;

- to ensure a competent and confident workforce;

- to review and, if necessary, to modernise legislation.

(Scottish Executive 2006a, p7).

The rationale for the review has already been referred to above and the review report notes a number of trends within society which will have an impact upon social work serv-ices. These include an increasingly ageing population juxtaposed with a decreasing child population which is likely to be in greater need, differences in the types of need requiring effective responses, increasing complexity within the context of social life, relationships and networks, increasing polarity between the affluent and the poor, a shrinking workforce, increasing cultural diversity, greater demands from the public for choice, independence and personalisation, advances in technology and an increasing need to ensure that services are regulated and integrated (Scottish Executive 2006a, pp17–22), taking into account the needs of all relevant stakeholders. The following quotation perhaps sums this up:

> *Social work is life-changing work. But now, at the start of the 21st century, social work itself needs to change so that it can match our country's expectations for high quality, accessible, responsive and personalised services.* (Roe, in Scottish Executive 2006a, p2)

The review of social work was just that: a review into all aspects and areas of social work relating to community care, criminal justice and work with children, young people and their families and of those services provided by local authorities or commissioned by them from voluntary and private-sector providers. The review also took account of the need to consider the role of social work *per se*, the role of the social worker within that and a number of other significant issues. This was a clear and conscious decision in order that, apart from anything else, the very interconnectedness of the social work task could be illuminated and referred to in order that the review and its findings might usefully inform the way future services are designed, configured, planned, implemented and evaluated, taking into account the whole person and their context.

RESEARCH SUMMARY

The review points to three main conclusions which its consultations have highlighted and which reflect the particular context for 21st century social work:

- *Doing more of the same won't work. Increasing demand, greater complexity and rising expectations mean that the current situation is not sustainable.*

- *Social work services don't have all of the answers. They need to work closely with other universal providers in all sectors to find new ways to design and deliver services across the public sector.*

- *Social workers' skills are highly valued and increasingly relevant to the changing needs of society. Yet we are far from making the best use of these skills.*

(Scottish Executive 2006a, p8)

These conclusions reflect a number of realities and have implications for the ways in which resources are utilised in the future. There is a shift in emphasis towards the social work task having as a focus capacity-building. This means that rather than simply delivering services to meet identified need, resources and services should be utilised in a way which also recognises the need for people to be active agents in promoting their own well-being in order that change becomes sustainable.

Refreshingly, it is concluded that social work really can't provide all of the answers to all of the problems in and of society. This has major implications for other public services and may well offer the opportunity for some honest dialogue about how best to integrate services effectively as well as raising the issues of accountability and transparency to new heights.

Continued ▷

And understandably, in my view, the skills of social workers are highly valued and increasingly relevant. This highlights the central importance to society of the social work role underpinned as it is by reference to core values, including:

- *respecting the right to self-determination;*
- *promoting participation;*
- *taking a whole-person approach;*
- *understanding each individual in the context of family and community;*
- *identifying and building on strengths.*

(Scottish Executive 2006a, p11)

However, it is also important to note that how those skills are utilised is likely to be the subject of much discussion in the future, with implications for employers and providers of qualifying and post-qualifying education programmes.

We shall now look at each of the six objectives referred to above in order that we can appreciate the significance of the issues considered by the review before looking at the main recommendations.

The role of the social worker and the social work profession

This was seen as a major priority for the review as the role of the social worker is fundamental to the profession and its task. In recent years there has been an increase in the number and diversity of roles undertaken by social workers, including those of advocate, counsellor, assessor, care manager and as an agent of social control (Scottish Executive 2005o) which had led people to question whether in fact social work continued to be a single profession. The review concluded:

> that it is and that it should remain a single, generic profession, underpinned by a common body of knowledge, skills and values, set out in the Framework for Social Work Education in Scotland. (Scottish Executive 2006a, p27).

The review also concluded that these roles are underpinned by knowledge, values and skills which are highly valued by both service users and other stakeholders (see above).

This gives a strong message that social work is what social work does and that despite the increasing specialisation of some services, the common knowledge base and those shared, core values and skills are crucially important and are a defining feature of social work as a profession. The specialisation of services reflects the capacity of the profession to respond to changes and challenges; diversity of role is something to be proud of and social work rises to this challenge well. What needs to underpin and reinforce this creativity is effective education, training and workforce development.

The issue regarding the importance of role and function is one which is most clearly apparent in those areas where there is a statutory element attached, for example in child care (Scottish Executive 2005l), mental health and criminal justice settings. However, the introduction of 'protection of title' means that only those people registered as a social worker with the SSSC can call themselves this and undertake such duties as are defined as being reserved for social workers (Scottish Executive 2005m). This represents a level of confirmation regarding the value of specialisation within social work which at the same time reinforces the need for such roles to be underpinned by expertise. The most vulnerable in society need reassurance that those people delivering services are those who are the best equipped to do so.

RESEARCH SUMMARY

Reserved functions of social workers

The primary reasons for setting out those functions which require to be designated as reserved to social workers is to safeguard people in certain circumstances and to protect their rights. A clear articulation of what it is only a social worker should do will also bring greater clarity to the roles they carry, particularly in integrated services. Once determined, these reserved functions should be set out in regulations.
(Scottish Executive 2005m, p4).

These functions can be grouped under the following headings:

- *Care and protection: only social workers should assess, subsequently plan and deliver the care to the most vulnerable people, including children, who are in need of protection from harm or who are at risk (see Chapter 4).*

- *Children who are looked after/accommodated: social workers should be responsible for making recommendations as to whether children should be accommodated and provide relevant services, including throughcare and aftercare (see Chapter 5).*

- *Childcare provision: social workers should be responsible for providing an appropriate service in relation to substitute care.*

- *Criminal justice: social workers should provide reports to the courts etc., and devise appropriate care plans.*

- *Mental health and incapacity: social workers should be responsible for the exercise of functions under the terms of the Mental Health (Care and Treatment) (S) Act 2003 and the Adults with Incapacity (S) Act 2000 (Patrick and Ward 2001).*

The whole issue of the role of social work and social workers is similarly informed by reference to issues around the very need for social work intervention (Scottish Executive 2005n) and the best way to ensure that services are delivered effectively at the front line (Scottish Executive 2005p) by practitioners who are doing what they have been trained to do (Scottish Executive 2005q). Figure 7.1 below offers a means of appreciating how the role of the social worker can differ depending upon the tasks needing to be undertaken.

Figure 7.1 illustrates how the social worker, the social work task, other service providers and, importantly, the community and volunteers all interrelate, interact and inform each other up to the point where increasing levels of need and risk point to the need for increasing specialisation in terms of service delivery. These tiers represent differing types of relationships between professionals and the public and demand from each particular skill which changes as the level of need and risk increases (see Chapter 3). The skills of the social worker are seen as being as much about direct engagement with others as they are about building the capacity or capabilities of people and communities to sustain changes and improvements in their lives. In this regard I see there being a need for social workers and other professionals to revisit the importance of learning theories, which have the potential to make sustainable change in people's lives a reality and offer social workers and others an effective tool to assist in building capacity. The box below considers some of the main issues relating to this.

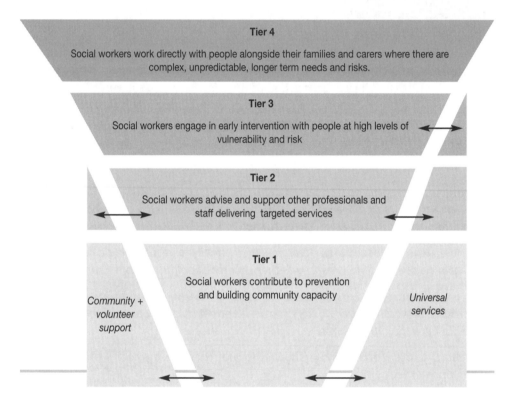

Figure 7.1 *The social worker's role: a tiered approach*

Source: Scottish Executive (2006b, p16)

Reproduced under the terms of Crown Copyright Policy Guidance issued by HMSO.

BUILDING CAPACITY TO SUSTAIN CHANGE: THE ROLE OF LEARNING?

Much is said about the importance of teaching and learning for social workers and other professionals, and Changing lives *makes many references to this important issue. However, what is often not made explicit is the importance of effective teaching by professionals to enhance the learning of service users in order that positive change might be more effectively sustained. In order to build capacity, we need to equip people with the skills and the tools to enable them to do this and I see a particular role for professionals in delivering services which not only meet the need for something in the here and now*

Continued

but which leave people with the benefit of the experience and new skills with which to sustain change thereafter.

In the context of service delivery to children, young people and their families, the role of teaching and learning has to be considered if change is to be sustainable. This refers to the use of effective teaching strategies by professionals to promote effective and sustainable learning by service users who can then hopefully use this to sustain positive change. Delivering a service is a potential learning situation for all concerned and that must now be a prime consideration. With that recognition comes the need for professionals to apply theory to their practice in order to enhance the learning that takes place within that context so that change is likely to be meaningful and sustainable.

What we do with children, young people and their families must be sustainable. Working with a parent to develop their parenting skills where neglect is an issue is a crucial piece of work. If you as a worker approach this with the wrong emphasis upon the role of teaching and learning, your intervention may well be ineffective. Many workers will bemoan what appears to be a lack of progress in childcare situations and may put this down to a number of things, including a lack of interest or ability on the part of the parent. However, have you considered how you are approaching this from a learning perspective? Have you identified the particular learning style of the parent/child? What type of teaching is more likely to result in effective learning, and therefore success, and how do you know when it has taken place? (Hothersall 2005; Knowles 1990; Kolb 1984; Saljo 1979; Schön 1987; Wenger 2000). These and other factors need to be considered if we are to deliver services which aim to promote sustainability. It is therefore necessary to remember that there are two distinct types of learning: surface learning, which refers to a quantitative increase in knowledge, the storing and memorising of information and the acquisition of facts; and deep learning, which refers to learning that allows people to make sense of what they are doing and understanding the reasons for it. In order for change to be sustainable, both types of learning need to be promoted, one preceding the other. The principles of both pedagogy and andragogy need to be utilised. If interventions do not address these issues explicitly, then the likelihood of sustainability is greatly reduced.

In this way, service users become active participants in their own learning and this involves them in service design and delivery in a meaningful way.

Organising and delivering social work services

Effective social work services promote independence and resilience, enabling some of our most vulnerable, excluded and even dangerous people to play an active part in society, through achieving change. (Scottish Executive 2006a, p17).

In a complex world, services tend to be complex, which can create problems not only for the recipients, but for the providers too. More and more services are seen to be integrated, arising as an amalgam of organisations, agencies and professionals. An integrated child and adolescent mental health team may well comprise social workers, psychiatrists, nurses, occupational therapists and psychotherapists working from a base within the local community. As we saw in Chapter 6, these arrangements bring with them particular challenges and these need to be highlighted and responded to if the vision of seamless services is to be realised.

The National Health Service Reform (S) Act 2004, with its emphasis upon community health partnerships (see s.2 of the 2004 Act) and their new statutory duties to promote health and well-being, may be one way to facilitate more effective service organisation and delivery as well as offering a framework within which some of the reserved functions of the social worker may well be carried out. Another opportunity which exists to facilitate more effective service design, delivery and implementation is the review of children's services and the children's hearing system with its focus upon early intervention and integrated assessment (Scottish Executive 2005a, 2005d).

The recommendations of the review concerning the organisation and delivery of services will provide the foundations for more personalised services including:

- *A greater focus on prevention*

- *Approaches to delivery across the public sector and partners in the voluntary and private sectors*

- *Flexible service delivery*

- *More effective use of social work skills*

- *More empowered users of services and*

- *Increased community capacity.*

(Scottish Executive 2006a, p33)

New legislation may also be produced (see below).

Quality assurance

Fundamental to any service system is the need for it to do what it should do as safely and effectively as possible. Quality services do not just mean value for money, although that is important. Social work and its related services are those which serve some of the most vulnerable people in society so they must be safe to use, easy to access, flexible and sensitive. The Social Work Inspection Agency (SWIA 2006) is one means by which and through which service standards can be monitored along with reference to the various service standards which now exist as well as the (Scottish) Standards in Social Work Education. Having quality services is dependent upon having quality staff and the new regulatory frameworks currently in existence were endorsed by the review.

A confident and competent workforce

As a student of the art and craft of social work, your training will equip you well. A clearly articulated set of common values, the eclectic nature of the knowledge base as well as the broad and transferable skill base you will acquire all contribute to your competence and confidence, which in its turn gives confidence to the public and other professionals in the integrity and value of the social work profession, its role and task. However, high-quality pre-registration training is only the beginning; once registered you have to continue your development and ensure that your knowledge, values and skills are regularly reviewed and updated. In fact, there is now a requirement for all registered social workers to undertake a basic minimum of post-registration training in order to be eligible for re-registration. These developmental requirements impose responsibilities upon individual workers and their employers (ADSW 2005; Scottish Executive 2005k; Skinner 2005).

The review makes reference in one of its three main conclusions (see above) to the view that social work skills are not being used as effectively as possible. Addressing this issue means that the whole of the social services workforce, seen by the review as including 'social workers, occupational therapists and other professionals, social work and occupational therapy assistants, care workers, residential care staff and support staff' (Scottish Executive 2006a, p7), must be utilised effectively. One suggestion is the development of a new paraprofessional role to work alongside social workers and other professionals in managing cases which would be a skilled role, nationally accredited. These and other suggestions reinforce the view that workforce development and planning, at pre- and post-qualifying levels, incorporating continuous professional and employee development, underpin many, if not all, of the many recommendations and suggestions of the review, and to some extent the continued development and existence of social work itself. In this way, the capacity of the profession is enhanced to continue to rise to new challenges. Furthermore, the importance of the interrelationship between theory and practice must be emphasised within all forms of training and education with an emphasis being placed upon inter-professional education (Colyer et al. 2005).

Leadership and management

Social work tends to operate within bureaucratic structures with formal and hierarchical line-management structures. These arrangements can have a disempowering effect upon social workers who can feel overly constrained in terms of their capacity to exercise professional judgement and in their ability to access resources, sometimes of the simplest sort, often because of the need to adhere to a multitude of procedures. Clearly, there are procedures which are vitally important (child protection procedures, for example) but there are those which are organisation or agency specific and may in fact not allow practitioners to work to their fullest potential. It is therefore important for service leaders and managers to lead and manage in ways which are empowering and are located at the vanguard of facilitating the development of services which are needs-led and responsive, underpinned by reference to ethically-sound practice. The review is considering how best to promote and support creative leadership with 21st century public service provision being clearly located within a framework of good governance and accountability (OPM/CIPFA 2004).

Issues around leadership and management are seen as being fundamental to sustaining change and developing capacity. The review emphasises the importance of effective leadership and good operational management.

Legislation

A major aspect of social work is the legislative base which underpins and surrounds it (Scottish Executive 2005r). As students of social work you have no doubt encountered lots of law during your studies and whilst on practice placements. There are many primary and secondary sources of legislation which have an effect upon your practice. There are also a number of other statutes relating to other professions which have a more indirect bearing upon what social work is and what social work does; health related legislation would be a good example of this. These may not appear to impinge upon the practitioner directly but in the world of integrated services the interface between these becomes all the more acute and at the strategic level such relationships are increasingly important and (probably)

21ST CENTURY SOCIAL WORK REVIEW: RECOMMENDATIONS

1. *Social work services must be designed and delivered around the needs of people who use services, their carers and communities.*

2. *Social work services must build individual, family and community capacity to meet their own needs.*

3. *Social work services must play a full and active part in a public sector wide approach to prevention and early intervention.*

4. *Social work services must become an integral part of a whole public sector approach to supporting vulnerable people and promoting social well-being.*

5. *Social work services must recognise and effectively manage the mixed economy of care in the delivery of services.*

6. *Social work services must develop a new organisational approach to managing risk, which ensures the delivery of safe, effective and innovative practice.*

7. *Employers must make sure that social workers are enabled and supported to practise accountably and exercise their professional autonomy.*

8. *Social work services must develop a learning culture that commits all individuals and organisations to lifelong learning and development.*

9. *Social work services should be delivered by effective teams designed to incorporate the appropriate mix of skills and expertise and operating with delegated authority and responsibilities.*

10. *Social work services must develop enabling leadership and effective management at all levels and across the system.*

11. *Social work services must be monitored and evaluated on the delivery of improved outcomes for people who use services, their carers and communities.*

12. *Social work services should develop the capacity and capability for transformational change by focusing on re-designing services and organisational development.*

13. *The Scottish Executive should consolidate in legislation the new direction of Scottish social work services.*

Reproduced from Changing lives: report of the 21st Century Social Work Review (Scottish Executive 2006a, pp91–4) under the terms of Crown Copyright Policy Guidance issued by HMSO

---

quite problematic. The review concluded that whilst new legislation was not required in order to implement its recommendations, such a development:

> *would make a powerful statement. It would set a landmark in the development of social work in Scotland, consolidating the significant changes we propose and laying the foundations for practice in the 21st century.* (Scottish Executive 2006a, p76)

The review felt that any new legislation should reflect more accurately the wider context of public service delivery, emphasising the importance of governance and the need to set out duties and expectations very clearly indeed. Other measures suggested relate to quality-assurance mechanisms, the maximisation of user involvement in service design and delivery, and mechanisms to develop social work practice. In relation to this last point, this might mean that continuous professional and employee development would have statutory significance. This would be a considerable boost to the profession, although the implications for HEIs, employers and employees would be significant.

The Scottish Executive has responded to the review's report (Scottish Executive 2006c) and make it clear that in their view the recommendations of *Changing lives* 'set social work services squarely in the context of the whole delivery of public services' (p5). Consistent with the Scottish Executive's aspirations for public services (Scottish Executive 2003d) to be joined up, personalised and focused on prevention and early intervention, the response document outlines six key responses which will assist in delivering the changes recommended by the review. These are:

- the development of national priorities for social work services;

- working towards transforming the way services are designed and delivered;

- strengthening the social work profession by reference to reserved functions, career pathways for social workers, more emphasis upon research and development activities and a clear framework of professional accountability;

- enhancing the capability of the profession by promoting a learning culture and empowering frontline staff to take decisions wherever they can, thus maximising the use of professional judgement;

- redefining the role of the Chief Social Work Officer to allow for more autonomy for frontline staff within a clear framework of governance and accountability;

- enabling and empowering leadership at all levels.

(Scottish Executive 2006c, pp8–13)

It has yet to be seen what effect the 21st Century Social Work Review will have. Much discussion and debate are now required on how the recommendations of the review can be taken forward. A ministerial group is to be established which will oversee developments and no doubt there will be consultation on the details of any proposed changes.

C H A P T E R   S U M M A R Y

This chapter has considered issues around the development of social work over the years and has focused upon the recent 21st Century Social Work Review, commenting upon the main recommendations and locating the issue of capacity building within a broad-based framework of learning.

FURTHER READING

Scottish Executive (2006) *Changing lives: report of the 21st Century Social Work Review*. Edinburgh: Scottish Executive. Available at www.scotland.gov.uk/Resource/Doc/91931/0021949.pdf

The report of the review group makes interesting reading.

Scottish Executive (2005) *The statutory social worker's role in prevention and early intervention with children*. Edinburgh: Scottish Executive.

Scottish Executive (2005) *The need for social work intervention*. Edinburgh: Scottish Executive.

Scottish Executive (2005) *The role of the social worker in the 21st century: a literature review*. Edinburgh: Edinburgh: Scottish Executive.

These supporting papers offer some useful material in relation to prevention and early intervention, the need for social work interventions and the role of the social worker.

References

Abbott, D, Watson, D and Townsley, R (2005) The proof of the pudding: what difference does multi-agency working make to families with disabled children with complex health care needs? *Child and Family Social Work*, 10 (3), 229–38.

Abrams, L (1998) *The orphan country*. Edinburgh: John Donald.

Adams, R, Dominelli, L and Payne, M (eds) (2005) *Social work futures: crossing boundaries, transforming practice.* Basingstoke: Palgrave Macmillan.

Alcock, P (2003) The subject of social policy, in Alcock, P, Erskine, A and May, M (eds): *The student's companion to social policy (2nd edition)*. Oxford: Blackwell.

Aldgate, J and Tunstill, J (1995) *Making sense of Section 17: implementing services for children in need within the Children Act 1989*. London: HMSO.

Alvesson, M (2003) *Understanding organisational culture*. London: Sage.

Arcelus, J, Bellerby, T and Vostanis, P (1999) A mental health service for young people in the care of the local authority, *Clinical Child Psychology and Psychiatry*, 4, 233–45.

Ashenden, S (2004) *Governing child sexual abuse: negotiating the boundaries of public and private, law and science.* London: Routledge.

Association of Directors of Social Work (ADSW) (2005) *Improving front line services: a framework for supporting front line staff*. Edinburgh: Scottish Executive.

Audit Scotland (2002) *Dealing with offending by young people*. Edinburgh: Audit Scotland.

Axford, N and Bullock, R (2005) *Child death and significant case reviews: internal approaches. Insight 19*. Edinburgh: Scottish Executive.

Bacon, H and Richardson, S (2001) 'Attachment theory and child abuse: an overview of the literature for practitioners', *Child Abuse Review*, 10, 377–97.

Baillie, D, Cameron, C, Cull, L-A, Roche, J and West, J (eds) (2003) *Social work and the law in Scotland*. Basingstoke: Palgrave Macmillan/Open University.

Bandura, A (1977) *Social learning theory*. Englewood Cliffs NJ: Prentice-Hall.

Barr, H (2003) *Interprofessional education: today, yesterday and tomorrow: a review.* Available at www.health.ltsn.ac.uk/miniprojects/HughBarrFinal.htm

Barrett, G and Keeping, C (2005) The process required for effective interprofessional working, in Barrett, G, Sellman, D and Thomas, J (eds) (2005), 18–32.

Barrett, G, Sellman, D and Thomas, J (eds) (2005) *Interprofessional working in health and social care: professional perspectives*. Basingstoke: Palgrave Macmillan.

Barron, RA, Byrne, D and Branscombe, NR (2006) *Social psychology (11th edition)*. Boston: Allyn and Bacon.

Barrows, P (1996) Individual psychotherapy for children in foster care: possibilities and limitations, *Clinical Child Psychology and Psychiatry*, 1, 385–97.

Becker, H (1963) *Outsiders: studies in the sociology of deviance*. New York. Free Press.

Bee, H and Boyd D (2003) *The developing child (10th edition)*. Boston MA: Allyn and Bacon.

Bell, M (1999) Working in partnership in child protection, *British Journal of Social Work*, 29, 437–55.

Beresford, P (2002) Making user involvement real, *Professional Social Work*, June, 16–17.

Berger, P and Luckman, T (1979) *The social construction of reality*. London: Peregrine Press/Penguin.

Berry, M, Charlson, R and Dawson, K (2003) Promising practices in understanding and treating child neglect, *Child and Family Social Work*, 8, 13–24.

Bertalanffy, V (1971) *General systems theory: foundations, development, application*. London: Allen Lane.

Biehal, N, Clayden, J, Stein, M and Wade, J (1992) *Prepared for living?* London: National Children's Bureau.

Biehal, N, Clayden, J, Stein, M and Wade, J (1995) *Moving on: young people and leaving care schemes.* London: HMSO.

Biestick, FP (1961) *The casework relationship*. London: Unwin.

Blom-Cooper, L (1985) *A child in trust. The report of the panel of inquiry into the circumstances surrounding the death of Jasmine Beckford.* London: Brent Council.

Bostock, L, Bairstow, S, Fish, S, and Macleod, F (2005) *Managing risk and minimising mistakes in services to children and families*. London: SCIE.

Bowlby, J (1997) *Attachment and loss.* Volume 1, *Attachment,* Volume 2, *Separation,* Volume 3, *Loss*. London: Pimlico.

Bradshaw, J (1972) The concept of social need, *New Society*, 30 March.

Brearley, CP (1982) *Risk in social work*. London: Routledge.

Bridges, W (2003) *Managing transitions: making the most of change*. London: Nicholas Brealey.

Briere, J (1992) *Child abuse trauma: theory and treatment of the lasting effects*. Newbury Park CA: Sage.

British Association of Social Workers (2002) *The code of ethics for social work.* Available at www.basw.co.uk/pages/info/ethics.htm

British Medical Association (BMA) (2004) *Handbook of ethics and law (2nd edition).* London: BMA. Available at: www.bma.org.uk/ap.nsf/Content/Hubethics

British Psychological Society (BPS) (2000) *Code of conduct, ethical principles and guidelines.* Available at www.bps.org.uk

British Sociological Society (2000) *Statement of ethical practice.* Available at britsoc.org.uk/about/ethic.htm

Broad, B (2001) Kinship care: supporting children in placements with extended family and friends, *Adoption and Fostering,* 25 (2), 33–41.

Bronfenbrenner, U (1979) *The ecology of human development.* Cambridge MA: Harvard University Press.

Bronfenbrenner, U (1986) Ecology of the family as a context for human development: research perspectives, *Developmental Psychology,* 22 (6), 723–42.

Bronfenbrenner, U (1989) Ecological systems theory, *Annals of Child Development,* 6, 187–249.

Brown, E, Bullock, R, Hobson, C and Little, M (1998) *Making residential care work: structure and culture in children's homes.* Aldershot: Ashgate.

Brown, L (2003) Mainstream or margin? The current use of family group conferences in child welfare practice in the UK, *Child and Family Social Work,* 8 (4), 331–40.

Browne, K and Lynch, M (1998) The challenge of child neglect, *Child Abuse Review,* 7, 73–6.

Browne, K and Saqi, S (1988) Approaches to screening for child abuse and neglect, in K Browne, C Davies and P Stratton (eds) *Early prediction and prevention of child abuse.* Chichester: John Wiley and Sons.

Buchanan, A (1999) Are care leavers significantly dissatisfied and depressed in adult life?, *Adoption and Fostering,* 23 (4), 35–40.

Buchanan, A (1996) *Cycles of child maltreatment: facts, fallacies and interventions.* Chichester: John Wiley and Sons.

Burford, G and Hudson, J (eds) (2000) *Family group conferencing: new directions in community-centred child and family practice.* New York: Aldine de Gruyter.

Butler, I (2002) A code of ethics for social work and social care research, *British Journal of Social Work,* 32, 239–48.

Butler, J and Vostanis, P (1998) Characteristics of referrals to a mental health service for young people in care, *Psychiatric Bulletin,* 22, 85–7.

Cairns, K (2002) *Attachment, trauma and resilience: therapeutic caring for children.* London: BAAF.

Calder, M and Hackett, S (eds) (2003) *Assessment in childcare: using and developing frameworks for practice.* Lyme Regis: Russell House.

Callaghan, J, Young, B, Richards, M and Vostanis, P (2003) Developing new mental health services for looked after children: a focus group study, *Adoption and Fostering,* 27 (4), 51–63.

Cartwright, R (2002) *Mastering team leadership*. Basingstoke: Palgrave Macmillan.

Cawson, P (2002) *Child maltreatment in the family: the evidence of a national sample of young people*. Leicester: NSPCC.

Cheung, SY and Buchanan, A (1997) Malaise scores in adulthood of children and young people who have been in care, *Journal of Child Psychology and Psychiatry*, 38, 575–80.

Clarke, J (1993) The comfort of strangers: social workers in context, in Clarke, J (ed.) *A crisis in care? Challenges to social work*. London: Sage.

Cleaver, H and Freeman, P (1995) *Parental perspectives in cases of suspected child abuse*. London: HMSO.

Cleaver, H and Freeman, P (1996) Suspected child abuse and neglect: are parents views important?, in Platt, D and Shemmings, P (eds) *Making enquiries into alleged child abuse and neglect: partnership with families.* London: John Wiley and Sons.

Clode, D (2003) *Integrated working and children's services: structures, outcomes and reform*. Available at www.integratedcarenetwork.gov.uk

Colyer, H, Helme, M and Jones, I (eds) (2005) *The theory–practice relationship in interprofessional education*. London: Higher Education Academy.

Cooke, P (1999) *Final report on disabled children and abuse*. Nottingham: The Ann Craft Trust.

Cooke, P and Standen, P (2002) Abuse and disabled children: hidden needs?, *Child Abuse Review*, 11, 1–18.

Cooper, A (2003) Risk and the framework for assessment, in M Calder and S Hackett (eds) *Assessment in child care: using and developing frameworks for practice*. Lyme Regis: Russell House.

Corby, B (2000) *Child abuse: towards a knowledge base (2nd edition)*. Maidenhead: Open University Press.

Corby, B, Doig, A and Roberts, V (2001) *Public inquiries into abuse of children in residential care*. London: Jessica Kingsley.

Cordess, C (ed.) (2001) *Confidentiality and mental health*. London: Jessica Kingsley.

Council of Europe (2003) *Convention for the Protection of Human Rights and Fundamental Freedoms*. Vilnius: Council of Europe.

Crawford, K and Walker, J (2003) *Social work and human development*. Exeter: Learning Matters.

Crittenden, P (1992) Children's strategies for coping with adverse home environments: an interpretation using attachment theory, *Child Abuse and Neglect*, 16 (3), 329–43.

Crittenden, P (1993) An information-processing perspective on the behaviour of neglectful parents, *Criminal Justice Behaviour*, 20, 27–48.

Crittenden, P (1997) Patterns of attachment and sexual behaviour: risk of dysfunction versus opportunity for creative integration, in Atkinson, L and Zucker, K (eds) *Attachment and psychopathology*. New York: Guilford Press.

Crittenden, P (1999) Child neglect: causes and contributors, H Dubowitz (ed.) *Neglected children: research, practice and policy*. Thousand Oaks CA: Sage.

Crittenden, P and Ainsworth, M (1989) Child maltreatment and attachment theory, in Cicchetti, D and Carlson, V (eds) *Child maltreatment: theory and research on the causes and consequences of child abuse and neglect*. New York: Cambridge University Press.

Dale, P (2004) 'Like a fish in a bowl': parents' perceptions of child protection services, *Child Abuse Review*, 13, 137–57.

Dalgleish, L (2003) Risk, needs and consequences, in Calder, M and Hackett, S (eds) *Assessment in child care: using and developing frameworks for practice*. Lyme Regis: Russell House.

Dalrymple, J and Horan, H (2003) Promoting the participation rights of children and young people in family group conferences, *Practice*, 15 (2), 5–14.

Daniel, B (2004) An overview of the Scottish multidisciplinary child protection review, *Child and Family Social Work*, 9, 247–57.

Daniel, B and Wassell, S (2002) *Assessing and promoting resilience in vulnerable children*, Volume 1, *The Early Years, Volume 2, The School Years, Volume 3, Adolescence*. London: Jessica Kingsley.

Department of Health (1988) *A guide for social workers undertaking a comprehensive assessment*. London: HMSO.

Department of Health (1995) *Child protection: messages from research*. London: HMSO.

Department of Health (2000) *The framework for the assessment of children in need and their families*. London: The Stationery Office.

Department of Health and Social Security (1974a) *Report of the Committee of Inquiry into the Care and Supervision Provided in Relation to Maria Colwell*. London: Department of Health and Social Security.

Department of Health and Social Security (1974b) *Non accidental injury to children*. LASSL (74) (13). London: Department of Health and Social Security.

Dimigen, G, Del Priore, C, Butler, S, Evans, S, Ferguson, L and Swan, M (1999) The need for a mental health service for children at commencement of being looked after and accommodated by the local authority: questionnaire survey, *British Medical Journal*, 319, 675.

Dingwall, R, Eekelaar, JM and Murray, T (1983) *The protection of children: state intervention and family life*. Oxford: Blackwell.

Dixon, J and Stein, M (2002) *Still a bairn: throughcare and aftercare services in Scotland*. Edinburgh: Scottish Executive. Available at www.scotland.gov.uk/library5/health/stillabairn.pdf

Doel, M and Marsh, P (1992) *Task centred social work*. Aldershot: Ashgate.

Dominelli, L (2002) *Feminist social work theory and practice*. Basingstoke: Palgrave Macmillan.

Donnison, DV (1954) *The neglected child and the social services*. Manchester: Manchester University Press.

Doyle, C (1997) *Working with abused children*. Basingstoke: Macmillan/BASW.

Drury-Hudson, J (1997) A model of professional knowledge for social work practice, *Australian Social Work*, 50, 35–44.

Dubowitz, H, Pitts, C, Litrownik, A, Cox, C, Runyon, D and Black, M (2005) Defining child neglect based on child protective services data, *Child Abuse and Neglect*, 29 (5), 493–511.

Egeland, B and Sroufe, L (1981) Attachment and early maltreatment, *Child Development*, 52, 44–52.

England, H (1986) *Social work as art*. London: Allen & Unwin.

Eysenck, M and Keane, M (2005) *Cognitive psychology*. New York: Madison Press.

Farmer, E and Owen, M (1995) *Child protection practice: private risks and public remedies: decision making, intervention and outcome in child protection work*. London: HMSO.

Ferguson, H (1997) Protecting children in need: child protection and the risk society, *Child and Family Social Work*, 2, 221–234.

Ferguson, H (2004) *Protecting children in time: child abuse, child protection and the consequences of modernity*. Basingstoke: Palgrave Macmillan.

Fionda, J (ed.) (2001) *Legal concepts of childhood*. Oxford: Hart.

Flavell, JH (1985) *Cognitive development*. Englewood Cliffs, NJ: Prentice-Hall.

Flexner, A (1915/2001) Is social work a profession?, *Research on Social Work Practice*, 11 (2), 152–165.

Fonagy, P, Steele, M, Steele, H, Higgitt, A and Target, M (1994) The theory and practice of resilience, *Journal of Child Psychology and Psychiatry*, 35 (2), 231–55.

Fook, J (2002) *Social work: critical theory and practice*. London: Sage.

Fostering Network (2005) *Caring for our children*. The Fostering Network. Available at www.thefostering.net/scotland/caring_for_our_children/

Foucault, M (1991) Governmentality, in Burchell, G, Gordon, C and Miller, P (eds) *The Foucault effect: studies in governmentality*. Hemel Hempstead: Harvester Wheatsheaf.

Fox-Harding, L (1997) *Perspectives in child care policy*. London: Longman.

Fraser, D (2003) *The evolution of the British welfare state (3rd edition)*. Basingstoke: Palgrave Macmillan.

Freeman, M (1983) Freedom and the welfare state: child-rearing, parental autonomy and state intervention, *Journal of Social Welfare Law*, March.

Freud, S (1991) *Introductory lectures on psychoanalysis*. Harmondsworth: Penguin.

Garbarino, J, Guttmann, E and Seeley, J (1986) *The psychologically battered child*. San Francisco: Jossey-Bass.

Garland, D (1990) Frameworks of inquiry in the sociology of punishment, *British Journal of Sociology*, 41 (1), 1–15.

General Teaching Council for Scotland (GTCS) (2002) *General code of practice*. Edinburgh: GTCS.

Germain, CB and Gitterman, A (1980) *The life model of social work practice*. New York: Columbia University Press.

Germain, CB and Gitterman, A (1996) *The life model of social work practice: advances in theory and practice (2nd edition)*. New York: Columbia University Press.

Ghate, D (2002) *Parenting in poor environments*. London: Jessica Kingsley.

Giddens, A (2001) *Sociology (4th edition)*. Cambridge: Polity Press.

Gilligan, R (1999) Working with social networks: key resources in helping children at risk, in Hill, M (ed.) *Effective ways of working with children and families*. London: Jessica Kingsley.

Gilligan, R (2000) Promoting resilience in children in foster care, in Gilligan, R and Kelly, G (eds) *Issues in foster care*. London: Jessica Kingsley.

Golding, K (2003) Helping foster carers helping children: using attachment theory to guide practice, *Adoption and Fostering*, 27 (2), 64–73.

Goldstein, EG (1973) *Social work practice: a unitary approach*. Columbia: University of South Carolina Press.

Goldstein, J, Freud, A and Solnit, A (1979) *Before the best interests of the child*. London: Free Press.

Göpfert, M, Webster, J and Seeman, MV (2000) *Parental psychiatric disorder: distressed parents and their families*. Cambridge: Cambridge University Press.

Hagell, A (1998) *Dangerous care: reviewing the risks to children from their carers*. London: Policy Studies Institute/Bridge Child Care Development Service.

Hammond, H (2001) *Child protection inquiry into the circumstances surrounding the death of Kennedy McFarlane (17/4/97)*. Dumfries and Galloway Child Protection Committee.

Hammond, KR (1996) *Human judgement and social policy: irreducible uncertainty, inevitable error, unavoidable injustice*. New York: Oxford University Press.

Hammond, KR, Hamm, RM, Grassia, J and Pearson, T (1987) Direct comparison of the efficacy of intuitive and analytical cognition in expert judgement, *IEE Transactions on Systems, Man and Cybernetics SMC*, 17 (5), 753–70.

Haralambos, M and Holborn, M (2004) *Sociology: themes and perspectives*. London: Collins.

Harbin, F and Murphy, M (eds) (2000) *Substance misuse and childcare*. Lyme Regis. Russell House.

Häring, B (1972) *Medical ethics*. Slough: St Paul. Cited Butler, I (2002) A code of ethics for social work and social care research, in *British Journal of Social Work*, 32, 239–48.

Harman, J, Childs, G and Kelleher, K (2000) Mental health care utilisation and expenditures by children in foster care, *Archives of Pediatric Adolescent Medicine*, 154, 1114–17.

Hatfield, B, Harrington, R and Mohamad, H (1996) Staff looking after children in local authority residential units: interface with child mental health professionals, *Journal of Adolescence*, 19, 127–39.

Hazler, RJ and Barwick N (2001) *The therapeutic environment*. Buckingham: Open University Press.

Healy, J (2002) *Social work practices: contemporary perspectives on change*. London: Sage.

Healy, K (2005) *Social work theories in context: creating frameworks for practice*. Basingstoke: Palgrave Macmillan.

Heath, AF, Colton, M and Aldgate, J (1989) The education of children in and out of care, *British Journal of Social Work*, 19, 447–60.

Heath, AF, Colton, MJ and Aldgate, J (1994) Failure to escape: a longitudinal study of foster children's educational achievement, *British Journal of Social Work*, 24, 241–60.

Herzberg, F (1968) One more time: how do you motivate employees?, *Harvard Business Review*, 46, 53–62.

HMI/SWSI (2001) *Learning with care: the education of children looked after away from home by local authorities*. Edinburgh: HMI/SWSI.

Holland, S, Faulkner, A and Perez-del-Aguila, R (2005) Promoting stability and continuity of care for looked after children: a survey and critical perspective, *Child and Family Social Work*, 10 (1), 29–41.

Hollows, A (2003) Making professional judgements in the framework for the assessment of children in need and their families, in Calder, M and Hackett, S (eds) *Assessment in child care: using and developing frameworks for practice*. Lyme Regis: Russell House.

Homan, R (1991) *The ethics of social research*. London: Longman. Cited in Butler, I (2002) A code of ethics for social work and social care research, *British Journal of Social Work*, 32, 239–48.

Home Office (1945) *The Monckton Report*. London: HMSO.

Horner, N (2003) *What is social work? Context and perspectives*. Exeter: Learning Matters.

Horwarth, J (ed.) (2001) *The child's world: assessing children in need*. London: Jessica Kingsley.

Horwarth, J and Shardlow, S (2003) *Making links across specialisms: understanding modern social work practice*. Lyme Regis: Russell House.

Hothersall, SJ (2005) Adult learning in social work practice. Unpublished paper. School of Applied Social Studies, The Robert Gordon University, Aberdeen.

Howe, D (1992) Child abuse and the bureaucratisation of social work, *The Sociological Review*, 14 (3), 1–10.

Howe, D (2005) *Child abuse and neglect: attachment, development and intervention*. Basingstoke: Palgrave Macmillan.

Hudson, B (1987) Collaboration in social welfare: a framework for analysis, *Policy and Politics,* 15 (3), 175–82.

Hudson, B (2002) Interprofessionality in health and social care, *Journal of Interprofessional Care*, 16 (1), 7–17.

Inglehart, AP (1994) Kinship foster care placement service and outcome issues, *Children and Youth Services Review*, 16, 107–22.

Ironside, L (2004) Living a provisional existence: thinking about foster carers and the emotional containment of children placed in their care, *Adoption and Fostering* 28 (4), 39–49.

Iwaniec, D (1995) *The emotionally abused and neglected child*. Chichester. John Wiley and Sons.

Iwaniec, D (1997) An overview of emotional maltreatment and failure to thrive, *Child Abuse Review*, 6, 370–88.

Iwaniec, D and Herbert, M (1999) Multi-dimensional approach to helping emotionally abused and neglected children and abusive parents, *Children and Society*, 13, 365–79.

Jack, G (2000) Ecological influences on parenting and child development, *British Journal of Social Work*, 30, 703–20.

Jackson, M (1988) The rediscovery of restrictions, *Policy and Politics* 16 (4), 277–83.

Jackson, S (1987) *The education of children in care*. University of Bristol, School of Applied Social Studies.

Jackson, S (1989) Residential care and education, *Children and Society,* 4, 335–50.

Jackson, S and Thomas, N (1999) *On the move again: what works in creating stability for looked after children?* Ilford: Barnardo's.

James, A and Prout, A (eds) (2003) *Constructing and reconstructing childhood (2nd edition)*. London: Routledge Falmer.

Jamieson, C (2002) Foreword, in Scottish Executive (2002a) *Scotland's Action Programme to Reduce Youth Crime*. Edinburgh: Scottish Executive, p2.

Jewett, C (1984) *Helping children cope with separation and loss*. London: Batsford.

Johns, R (2005) *Using the law in social work (2nd edition)*. Exeter: Learning Matters.

Kempe, CH, Silverman, FN, Steele, BF, Droegemueller, W and Silver, HK (1962) The battered child syndrome, *Journal of the American Medical Association*, 181 (1), 17–24.

Kendall-Tackett, K (2002) The health effects of childhood abuse: four pathways by which abuse can influence health, *Child Abuse and Neglect*, 26, 715–29.

Kendall-Tackett, K and Eckenrode, J (1996) The effects of neglect on academic achievement and disciplinary problems: a developmental perspective, *Child Abuse and Neglect*, 20, 161–9.

Kendrick, A (2002) Close enough? Professional closeness and safe caring, *Scottish Journal of Residential Child Care*, 1, 46–54.

Kendrick, A and Fraser, S (1992) Summary of literature review on residential child care, in SWSI (1992) *Another kind of home: a review of residential child care*. Edinburgh: The Scottish Office.

Kennedy, M (1995) Perceptions of abused disabled children, in Wilson, K and James, A (eds) *The child protection handbook*. London: Bailliere Tindall, 127–49.

Kent, R (1997) *Children's safeguards review.* Edinburgh: The Stationery Office.

Klahr, D (1992) Information-processing approaches to cognitive development, in Bernstein, M and Lamb, M (eds) *Developmental psychology: an advanced textbook (3rd edition)*. Hillsdale NJ: Erlbaum.

Knowles, MS (1990) *The adult learner: a neglected species (4th edition)*. Houston TX: Gulf Publishing.

Kolb, DA (1984) *Experiential learning: experience as the source of learning and development*. London: Prentice Hall.

Koprowska, J (2005) *Communication and interpersonal skills in social work*. Exeter: Learning Matters.

Kuhn, T (1962) *The structure of scientific revolutions*. Chicago: University of Chicago Press.

Laming, H (2003) *The Victoria Climbié inquiry*. London: The Stationery Office.

Lehner, K (2003) The role of primary care trusts in promoting the health needs of looked after children, *Adoption and Fostering*, 27 (3), 79–81.

Lewin, K (1997) Behaviour and development as a function of the total situation, Lewin, G and Cartwright, D (eds) *Resolving social conflicts and field theory in social science*. Washington DC: American Psychological Association.

Lishman, J (2005) The case for change. Unpublished Paper. School of Applied Social Studies, The Robert Gordon University, Aberdeen.

Lupton, D (1999) *Risk*. London: Routledge.

Macaskill, C (2002) *Safe contact?, Children in permanent placement and contact with their birth relatives*. Lyme Regis: Russell House.

MacKenzie, WJM (1969) *Social work in Scotland: report of a working party on the Social Work (Scotland) Act 1968*. Edinburgh: University of Edinburgh.

Maclean, K (2002) Two and a half cheers for the National Care Standards, *Scottish Journal of Residential Child Care*, 1, 41–2.

Maclean, K and Gunion, M (2003) Learning with care: the education of children looked after away from home by local authorities in Scotland, *Adoption and Fostering*, 27 (2), 20–31.

Marsh, P and Crow, G (1997) *Family and group conferences in child welfare*. Oxford: Blackwell.

Maslow, A (1970) *Motivation and personality (2nd edition)*. New York: Harper and Row.

Mather, M and Humphrey, J (1997) The statutory medical and health needs of looked after children: time for a radical review?', *Adoption & Fostering*, 21 (2), 36–40.

McBoyle, J (1963) *Working together: problem families*. RIPA Conference Proceedings: Peebles.

McCann, JB, James, A, Wilson, S and Dunn, G (1996) Prevalence of psychiatric disorders in young people in the care system, *British Medical Journal*, 1529–30.

McElrea, JFWM (1998) The New Zealand model of family group conferencing, *European Journal on Criminal Policy and Research*, 6 (4), 527–43.

McGhee, J and Francis, J (2003) Protecting children in Scotland: examining the impact of the Children (Scotland) Act 1995, *Child and Family Social Work*, 8, 133–42.

McNorrie, K McK (1998) *The Children (Scotland) Act 1995 (2nd edition)*. Green's Annotated Acts. Edinburgh: W. Green and Sons.

McNorrie, K McK (2005) *Children's hearings in Scotland (2nd edition)*. Edinburgh: W. Green and Sons.

Mead, GH (1934) *Mind, self and society*. London: University of Chicago Press.

Meltzer, H, Gatward, R, Goodman, R and Ford, T (2000) *Mental health of children and adolescents in Great Britain*. London: TSO.

Meltzer, H, Lader, D, Corbin, T, Goodman, R and Ford, T (2004) *The mental health of young people looked after by local authorities in Scotland: summary report*. Norwich: HMSO.

Miller, C, Freeman, M and Ross, N (2001) *Interprofessional practice in health and social care*. London: Arnold.

Millham, S, Bullock, R, Hosie, K and Haak, M (1986) *Lost in care*. Aldershot: Gower.

Minnis, H and Del Priore, C (2001) Mental health services for looked after children: implications from two studies, *Adoption and Fostering* 25 (4), 27–38.

Moore, B (1996) *Risk assessment: a practitioners guide to predicting harmful behaviour*. London: Whiting and Birch.

Mullender, A, Hague, G, Imam, U, Kelly, L, Malos, E and Regan, L (2002) *Children's perspectives on domestic violence*. London: Sage.

Murphy, J. (1992) *British social services: the Scottish dimension*. Edinburgh: Scottish Academic Press.

National Audit Office (2005) *Working with the third sector*. London: National Audit Office.

Neil, E (2000) The reasons why young children are placed for adoption: findings from a recently placed sample and a discussion of implications for subsequent identity development, *Child and Family Social Work*, 5, 303–16.

NESCPC (2004) *Child protection guidelines*. NESCPC. Available at www.nescpc.org.uk/nescpc/CPguidelines.pdf

Newman, T and Blackburn, S (2002) *Transitions in the lives of children and young people: resilience factors.* Edinburgh: Scottish Executive Education Department.

Nicol, R, Stretch, D, Whitney, I, Jones, K, Garfield, P, Turner, K and Stanion, B (2000) Mental health needs and services for severely troubled and troubling young people, including young offenders in an NHS region, *Journal of Adolescence*, 23, 243–61.

Nursing and Midwifery Council (NMC) (2002) *Code of professional conduct*. London: NMC.

O'Brien, S, Hammond, H and McKinnon, M (2003) *Report of the Caleb Ness inquiry*. Edinburgh and Lothians Child Protection Committee.

Office of Public Management/Chartered Institute of Public Finance and Accountancy (OPM/CIPFA) (2004) *The good governance standard for public services*. London: OPM/CIPFA.

O'Hagan, K (1993) *Emotional and psychological abuse of children*. Milton Keynes: Open University Press.

Øvretveit, J (1997) How to describe interprofessional working, in Øvretveit, J, Mathias, P and Thompson, T (1997), 9–33.

Øvretveit, J, Mathias, P and Thompson, T (eds) (1997) *Interprofessional working for health and social care*. London: Macmillan.

Parker, J and Bradley, G (2003) *Social work practice: assessment, planning, intervention and review*. Exeter: Learning Matters.

Patrick, H and Ward, A (2001) *Mental Health (S) Act 1984 and Adults with Incapacity (S) Act 2000*. Greens Annotated Acts. Edinburgh: W.Green and Sons.

Payne, H (2000) The health of children in public care, *Child and Adolescent Mental Health*, 8, 78–83.

Payne, M (1996) *What is professional social work?* Birmingham: Venture Press/BASW.

Payne, M (2000) *Teamwork in multiprofessional care*. Basingstoke: Palgrave Macmillan.

Payne, M (2005) *Modern social work theory (3rd edition)*. Basingstoke: Palgrave Macmillan.

Payne, M and Shardlow, S (eds) (2002) *Social work in the British Isles*. London: Jessica Kingsley.

Piaget, J and Inhelder, B (1969) *The psychology of the child*. New York: Basic Books.

Pincus, A and Minahan, A (1973) *Social work practice: model and method*. Itasca Il: Peacock.

Pollard, K, Sellman, D and Senior, B (2005) The need for interprofessional working, in Barrett, G, Sellman, D and Thomas, J (eds) *Interprofessional working in health and social care: professional perspectives*. Basingstoke: Palgrave Macmillan, 7–17.

Polnay, L and Ward, H (2000) Promoting the health of looked after children, *British Medical Journal,* 320, 661–662.

Quinney, A (2006) *Collaborative social work practice*. Exeter: Learning Matters.

Quinton, D and Rutter, M (1984) Parents with children in care – II intergenerational continuities, *Journal of Child Psychology and Psychiatry*, 25, 231–50.

Quinton, D, Rushton, A, Dance, C and Mayes, D (1998) *Joining new families: a study of adoption and fostering in middle childhood*. Chichester: John Wiley and Sons.

Reder, P and Duncan, S (1999) *Lost innocents: a follow-up study of fatal child abuse*. London: Routledge.

Reder, P and Duncan, S (2003) Understanding communication in child protection networks, in *Child Abuse Review*, 12, 82–100.

Reder, P, Duncan, S and Gray, M (1993) *Beyond blame: child abuse tragedies revisited*. London: Routledge.

Richardson, J and Joughin, C (2000) *The mental health needs of looked after children*. London: Gaskell.

Richardson, N (2005) *Social costs: the effects of child maltreatment*. Melbourne: The National Child Protection Clearing House.

Richardson, S and Bacon, H (eds) (2001) *Creative responses to child sexual abuse: challenges and dilemmas*. London: Jessica Kingsley.

Roberts, AR (ed.) (2000) *Crisis intervention handbook (2nd edition)*. New York: Oxford University Press.

Rowe, J, Cain, H, Hundleby, M and Keane, A (1984) *Long-term foster care*. London: Batsford/BAAF.

Rowntree, BS (1901) *Poverty: a study of town life*. Basingstoke: Macmillan.

Rutter, M (1985) Resilience in the face of adversity, *British Journal of Psychiatry*, 147, 598–611.

Rutter, M (1995) Psychosocial adversity: risk, resilience and recovery, *Southern African Journal of Child and Adolescent Psychiatry*, 7 (2), 75–88.

Rutter, M, Giller, G and Hagell, A (1998) *Antisocial behaviour by young people*. Cambridge: Cambridge University Press.

Ryburn, M (1998) A new model of welfare: re-asserting the value of kinship for children in state care, *Social Policy and Administration*, 32 (1), 28–45.

Saljo, R (1979) *Learning in the learners perspective: some common place misconceptions*. Gothenburg: University of Gothenburg.

Samra-Tibbets, C and Raynes, B (1999) Assessment and planning in Calder, M and Horwarth, J (eds) *Working for children on the child protection register*. Aldershot: Arena.

Scannapieco, M (1999) Kinship care in the public child welfare system: a systematic review of the research, in Hegar, RL and Scannapieco, M (eds) *Kinship foster care: policy, practice and research*. Oxford: Oxford University Press, 141–54.

Schofield, G (2001) Resilience and family placement: a lifespan perspective, *Adoption and Fostering*, 25 (3), 7–19.

Schön, D (1987) *Educating the reflective practitioner*. London: Jossey Bass.

Scott, G, Mooney, G and Brown, U (2005) Managing poverty in the devolved Scotland, in Mooney, G and Scott, G (eds) *Exploring social policy in the 'New' Scotland*. Bristol: Policy Press.

Scottish Executive (1998) *Deciding in children's interests*. Edinburgh: Scottish Executive.

Scottish Executive (1999) *Aiming for excellence: modernising social work services in Scotland*. Edinburgh: Scottish Executive.

Scottish Executive (2000) *It's a criminal waste: stop youth crime now*. Edinburgh: Scottish Executive.

Scottish Executive (2001a) *For Scotland's children: better integrated children's services*. Edinburgh: Scottish Executive.

Scottish Executive (2001b) *National programme for improving mental health and well-being*. Edinburgh: Scottish Executive.

Scottish Executive (2002a) *Scotland's action programme to reduce youth crime*. Edinburgh: Scottish Executive.

Scottish Executive (2002b) *National standards for Scotland's youth justice services*. Edinburgh: Scottish Executive.

Scottish Executive (2002c) *Disciplining children: research with parents in Scotland*. Edinburgh: Scottish Executive.

Scottish Executive (2002d) *It's everyone's job to make sure I'm alright: literature review*. Edinburgh: Scottish Executive.

Scottish Executive (2002e) *It's everyone's job to make sure I'm alright: report of the Child Protection Audit and Review*. Edinburgh: Scottish Executive.

Scottish Executive (2003a) *The framework for social work education in*

Scotland. Edinburgh: Scottish Executive.

Scottish Executive (2003b): *The children's hearing system in Scotland: training resource manual (2nd edition)*. Edinburgh: Scottish Executive.

Scottish Executive (2003c): *Getting our priorities right: good practice guidance for working with children and families affected by substance misuse*. Edinburgh: Scottish Executive.

Scottish Executive (2003d) *Partnerships for a better Scotland*. Edinburgh: Scottish Executive.

Scottish Executive (2004a) *Family matters: improving family law in Scotland*. Edinburgh: Scottish Executive.

Scottish Executive (2004b) *Guide to the Anti-Social Behaviour etc. (Scotland) Act 2004*. Edinburgh: Scottish Executive.

Scottish Executive (2004c) *Protecting children and young people: the charter.* Edinburgh: Scottish Executive.

Scottish Executive (2004d) *Protecting children and young people: framework for standards*. Edinburgh: Scottish Executive.

Scottish Executive (2004e) *Throughcare and aftercare of looked after children in Scotland*. Available at www.scotland.gov.uk/library5/education/tcac-03.asp

Scottish Executive (2004f) *Supporting young people leaving care in Scotland: regulations and guidance on services for young people ceasing to be looked after by local authorities*. Edinburgh: Scottish Executive.

Scottish Executive (2004g) *Pathways handbook*. Edinburgh: Scottish Executive.

Scottish Executive (2005a) *Getting it right for every child: proposals for action.* Edinburgh: Scottish Executive.

Scottish Executive (2005b) *Fast track children's hearings pilot: final report of the evaluation of the pilot*. Edinburgh: Scottish Executive.

Scottish Executive (2005c) *Evaluation of the hamilton sheriff youth court pilot 2003–2005. Research findings 80/2005*. Edinburgh: Scottish Executive.

Scottish Executive (2005d): *Getting it right for every child: supporting paper 1: the process and content of an integrated framework and the implications for implementation*. Edinburgh: Scottish Executive. Available at www.scotland.gov.uk/Publications/2005/07/25112327/23305

Scottish Executive (2005e) *Child protection committees*. Edinburgh: Scottish Executive.

Scottish Executive (2005f) *National care standards: foster care and family placement services*. Edinburgh: Scottish Executive.

Scottish Executive (2005g) *National care standards: care homes for children and young people*. Edinburgh: Scottish Executive.

Scottish Executive (2005h) *National care standards: school care accommodation services.* Edinburgh: Scottish Executive.

Scottish Executive (2005i) *National care standards: adoption agencies* (revised edition). Edinburgh: Scottish Executive.

Scottish Executive (2005j) *21st century social work review: interim report*. Available at www.21csocialwork.org.uk/documents/Reports/Interim%20Report.pdf

Scottish Executive (2005k) *National strategy for the development of the social service workforce in Scotland: a plan for action 2005–2010*. Edinburgh: Scottish Executive.

Scottish Executive (2005l) *The statutory social worker's role in prevention and early intervention with children*. Edinburgh: Scottish Executive.

Scottish Executive (2005m) *Reserved functions of the social worker.* Edinburgh: Scottish Executive.

Scottish Executive (2005n) *The need for social work intervention*. Edinburgh: Scottish Executive.

Scottish Executive (2005o) *The role of the social worker in the 21st century: a literature review*. Edinburgh: Scottish Executive.

Scottish Executive (2005p) *Delegation of authority nearer to frontline staff: a scoping paper*. Edinburgh: Scottish Executive.

Scottish Executive (2005q) *Time for work study*. Edinburgh: Scottish Executive.

Scottish Executive (2005r) *Social work related legislation in Scotland: a summary of current legislation*. Edinburgh: Scottish Executive.

Scottish Executive (2005s) *The mental health of children and young people: a framework for promotion, prevention and care.* Edinburgh: Scottish Executive.

Scottish Executive (2006a) *Changing lives: report of the 21st Century Social Work Review*. Edinburgh: Scottish Executive. Available at www.scotland.gov.uk/Resource/Doc/91931/0021949.pdf

Scottish Executive (2006b) *Changing lives: summary report of the 21st Century Social Work Review*. Edinburgh: Scottish Executive. Available at www.scotland.gov.uk/Resource/Doc/91949/0021950.pdf

Scottish Executive (2006c) *Changing lives: Scottish Exeutive response to the Report of the 21st Century Social Work Review*. Edinburgh: Scottish Executive. Available at www.scotland.gov.uk/Resource/Doc/92357/0022094.pdf

Scottish Home and Health Department and Scottish Education Department (1964) *Report on children and young persons, Scotland (Cmnd 2306) (The Kilbrandon Report)*. Edinburgh: SHHD and SED.

Scottish Home and Health Department and Scottish Education Department (1966) *Social work and the community (Cmnd 3065)*. Edinburgh: SHHD and SED.

Scottish Office (1992) *Another kind of home: a review of residential child care (The Skinner Report)*. Edinburgh: The Stationery Office.

Scottish Office (1997a) *Scotland's children. The Children (Scotland) Act 1995. Regulations and Guidance. Volume 1, Support and protection for children and their families.* Edinburgh: The Stationery Office.

Scottish Office (1997b) *Scotland's children. The Children (Scotland) Act 1995. Regulations and guidance. Volume 2, Children looked after by local authorities.* Edinburgh: The Stationery Office

Scottish Office (1997c) *Scotland's children. The Children (Scotland) Act 1995. Regulations and Guidance. Volume 3, Adoption and parental responsibilities orders.* Edinburgh: The Stationery Office.

Scottish Office (1997d) *Scotland's Children. The Children (Scotland) Act 1995. Regulations and Guidance. Volume 4, References and bibliography.* Edinburgh: The Stationery Office.

Scottish Office (1998) *Protecting children: a shared responsibility. Guidance on inter-agency co-operation.* Edinburgh: Scottish Office.

Scottish Social Services Council (2005) *Codes of practice for social service workers and employers.* Dundee: SSSC.

Scourfield, J (2000) The rediscovery of child neglect, *The Sociological Review,* 48 (3), 365–82.

Scourfield, J and Welsh, I (2003) Risk, reflexivity and social control in child protection: new times or same old story?, *Critical Social Policy,* 23 (3), 398–420.

Searle, JR (1995) *The construction of social reality.* London: Allen Lane/Penguin.

Semple, M and Cable, S (2003) The new code of professional conduct, *Nursing Standard,* 17 (23), 40–8.

Sewpaul, V (2005) Global standards: promise and pitfalls for re-inscribing social work into civil society, *International Journal of Social Welfare,* 14, 210–17.

Sheldon, B (1995) *Cognitive-behavioural therapy: research, practice and philosophy.* London: Routledge.

Sheppard, M and Woodcock, J (1999) Need as an operating concept: the case of social work with children and families, *Child and Family Social Work,* 4, 67–76.

Sidebotham, P (2000) Patterns of child abuse in early childhood: a cohort study of the 'Children of the Nineties', *Child Abuse Review,* 9, 311–20.

Sieppart, JD, Hudson, J and Unrau, Y (2000) Family group conferencing in child welfare: lessons from a demonstration project, *Families in Society,* 81 (4), 382–91.

Sinclair, R and Bullock, R (2002) *Learning from past experience: a review of serious case reviews.* London: Department of Health.

Skinner, BF (1980) *Notebooks* (edited by R Epstein). Englewood Cliffs NJ: Prentice-Hall.

Skinner, K (2005) *Continuing professional development for the social services workforce in Scotland*. Dundee: SIESWE.

Smith, P, Cowie, H and Blades, M (2003) *Understanding children's development (4th edition)*. Oxford: Blackwell.

Social Work Inspection Agency (SWIA) (2005) *An inspection into the care and protection of children in Eilean Siar*. Edinburgh: The Scottish Executive.

Social Work Inspection Agency (SWIA) (2006) *SWIA charter*. Available at: www.swia.gov.uk

Social Work Services Group (1993) *Scotland's children: proposals for child care policy and law*. Edinburgh: SWSG.

Scottish Work Services Inspectorate (SWSI) (1992) *Another kind of home: a review of residential child care*. Edinburgh: The Scottish Office.

Social Work Services Inspectorate (SWSI) (2004) *Investigations into Scottish Borders Council and NHS Borders Services for people with learning disabilities: joint statement from the Mental Welfare Commission and the Social Work Services Inspectorate*. Edinburgh: Scottish Executive.

Spratt, T (2001) The influence of child protection orientation on child welfare practice, *British Journal of Social Work*, 31, 933–54.

Stanley, N, Penhale, B, Riordan, D, Barbour, RS and Holden, S (2003) *Child protection and mental health services: interprofessional responses to the needs of mothers*. Bristol: Policy Press.

Statham, D (2004) The context for managing practice, in Statham, D (ed.) *Managing front-line practice in social care.* London: Jessica Kingsley.

Statham, J and Holtermann, S (2004) Families on the brink: the effectiveness of family support services, *Child and family social work,* 9, 153–66.

Stevenson, O (1998) Neglect: where now? some reflections, *Child Abuse Review*, 7, 111–15.

Stone, B (1998) Child neglect: practitioners perspectives, *Child Abuse Review*, 7, 87–96.

Strathdee, R and Johnson, M (1994) *Out of care and on the streets: young people, care leavers and homelessness*. London: Centrepoint.

Straus, M and Kantor, J (2005) Definition and measurement of neglectful behaviour: some principles and guidelines, *Child Abuse and Neglect*, 29 (5), 19–29.

Sundell, K and Vinnerljung, B (2004) Outcomes of family group conferencing in Sweden: A 3 year follow-up, *Child Abuse and Neglect*, 28, 267–87.

Tanner, K and Turney, D (2003) What do we know about child neglect? A critical review of the literature and its application to social work practice, *Child and Family Social Work*, 8, 25–34.

Thompson, N (2002) *People skills (2nd edition)*. Basingstoke: Palgrave Macmillan.

Thompson, N (2003) *Communication and language*. Basingstoke: Palgrave Macmillan.

Thompson, N (2005) *Understanding social work: preparing for practice (2nd edition)*. Basingstoke: Palgrave Macmillan.

Thorburn, J, Lewis, A and Shemmings, D (1995) *Paternalism or partnership? Family involvement in the child protection process*. London: HMSO.

Tietze, S, Cohen, L and Musson, G (2003) *Understanding organisations through language*. London: Sage.

Tisdall, E and Kay, M (1997) *The Children (Scotland) Act 1995. Developing policy and law for scotland's children*. Edinburgh: The Stationery Office.

Townsend, P (1979) *Poverty in the UK*. Harmondsworth: Penguin.

Trieschman, AE, Whittaker, JK and Brendtro, LK (1969) *The other 23 hours: child care work with emotionally disturbed children in a therapeutic milieu*. New York: Aldine de Gruyter.

Trotter, C (1999) *Working with involuntary clients*. London: Sage.

Tuckman, BW, and Jensen, MC (1977) Stages of small group development revisited, *Group and Organisational Studies*, 2, 419–27.

Turney, D and Tanner, K (2001) Working with neglected children and their families in *Journal of Social Work Practice*, 15 (2), 193–204.

United Nations (1985) *United nations standard minimum rules for the administration of juvenile justice (The Beijing Rules)*. Geneva: United Nations.

United Nations (1989) *The UN Convention on the Rights of the Child*. Geneva: United Nations.

Vygotsky, L. (1978): *Mind and society: the development of higher mental processes*. Cambridge: MA: Harvard University Press.

Walker, S and Beckett, C (2003) *Social work assessment and intervention*. Lyme Regis: Russell House.

Waterhouse, L, McGhee, J, Whyte, W, Loucks, N, Kay, H and Stewart, R (2000) *The evaluation of children's hearings in Scotland*. Edinburgh: Scottish Executive.

Watson, D (2003) Defining quality of care for looked after children: frontline workers perspectives on standards and all that?, *Child and Family Social Work*, 8, 67–77.

Weber, M (1946) *From Max Weber: essays in sociology*. London: Routledge and Kegan Paul.

Weinstein, J, Whittington, C and Leiba, T (eds) (2003) *Collaboration in social work practice*. London: Jessica Kingsley.

Wenger, E (2000) *Communities of practice*. Cambridge: Cambridge University Press.

Wheeler, P (2003) Shaken baby syndrome: an introduction to the literature,

Child Abuse Review, 12, 401–15.

Whittington, C (2003a) Collaboration and partnership in context, in Weinstein, J, Whittington, C and Leiba, T (eds) *Collaboration in social work practice*. London: Jessica Kingsley.

Whittington, C (2003b) *Learning for collaborative practice with other professions and agencies*. London: Department of Health.

Whyte, B (2004) Responding to youth crime in Scotland, *British Journal of Social Work*, 34, 395–411.

Wilkes, R (1981) *Social work with undervalued groups*. London: Tavistock Publications.

Wilson, K and Bell, M (2003) *An evaluation of family group conferences*. York: University of York.

Winnicott, DW (1958) *Through paediatrics to psychoanalysis*. London: Hogarth Press.

Wolock, I and Horowitz, B (1984) Child maltreatment as a social problem: the neglect of neglect, *American Journal of Orthopsychiatry*, 54, 530–43.

Woodhouse, D and Pengelly, P (1991) *Anxiety and the dynamics of collaboration*. Aberdeen: Aberdeen University Press.

Woods, ME and Hollis, F (1990) *Casework: a psychosocial approach, (4th edition)*. New York: McGraw-Hill.

Wood-Schneider, M, Ross, A, Graham, J and Zielinski, A (2005) Do allegations of emotional maltreatment predict developmental outcomes beyond that of other forms of maltreatment?, *Child Abuse and Neglect*, 29(5), 513–532.

World Health Organisation (2002) *World report on violence and health*. Geneva: World Health Organisation.

Zigler, E, Taussig, C and Black, K (1992) Early childhood intervention: a promising preventative for juvenile delinquency, *American Psychologist*, 47 (8), 997–1006

Index